An inside guide to U2 places and the stories behind them

by Dave Griffith

Where locations are private residences or are not open to the public, we particularly ask all readers to respect absolutely the privacy of those who live or work there.

Publisher: Mark Neeter
Editor: Matt Milton

For photo credits see www.redplanetzone.com

ISBN: 978 1 9059 5999 0

Printed in the UK by CPI

Contents

Acknowledgements

To my Dad, Harry (1945-2012). He had Bono stories before anyone else did.

I wish to gratefully acknowledge the help of Donncha O'Cróinín, Karen Willis and my father, Harry Griffith, for various read-throughs and checking facts: without their help this would be more than likely unreadable. And thanks to Elva Tarpey, whose memories of the TV Club, the Top Hat and the Baggot Inn in their heyday made great listening, let alone giving a few glimpses into these venues when they were still being used for music!

Thanks to Tom Roseingrave and Alan Oliver for additional research

To Donal Murphy, many thanks. This man's knowledge of both U2 and Cork were an invaluable resource.

Much appreciation to Alex Montcharles who spent some time showing me around the U2 spots of Slane Castle. And many thanks to Rhonda DePaor for organising the trip.

Thanks to Vicky Moran in RTÉ for double-checking a date or two for me. Also, thanks to Roisin Iremonger in the Gaiety Theatre who kindly arranged access to the stage to take a few shots.

Thanks to David Walsh, whose knowledge of the northside of Dublin helped a lot. And to Robin Ball of Fundamental Studios in Wicklow, who worked on the *Pop* album – cheers for the direction).

Dominic Doherty, Deputy Director of the Students Union in Queens University, Belfast deserves a big thank you for directions around the city, as well as for giving me background and access to where U2 played in the university.

Tracy O'Toole of the King's Hall in Belfast – thanks for checking the venue and dates for me. Jan Carson of the Ulster Hall – thanks for all the help.

I'd also like to thank Derek O'Mahony from Howth who helped me locate a few spots around the area. Last but not least, I also wish to thank all the tourists who weren't afraid to ask me questions – it's made my initial shortlist of U2-related places to see quite long. It was fun finding them, and I'm sure I still have plenty more to find...

A brief history of Dublin

Dublin – the capital city of Ireland – is on the east coast of the most western island of Europe. To the east of Ireland is Great Britain, separated by the Irish Sea. The island itself is divided between the Republic of Ireland, which covers just under five-sixths of the island, and Northern Ireland, a part of the United Kingdom, which covers the remainder and is located in the northeast of the island.

Although inhabited since around 8000BC, the city of Dublin itself was established by the Vikings around 988AD. The name Dublin derived from the Viking name Dyff Lynn (or Dubh Linn in modern Irish), meaning 'Black Pool' – named after a part of the River Liffey that appeared black, and which was a perfect spot for the Vikings to dock their ships. This 'Black Pool', although no longer anything like a pool, can be viewed in the grounds of Dublin Castle.

A community developed from around the quayside in the vicinity of where Christ Church Cathedral now stands, down as far as Dame Street (near Trinity College). A street off Dame Street called Suffolk Street is where the Vikings established their parliament in Dublin. The original boundary walls can be seen in the vicinity of Christ Church Cathedral and at the back of nearby St Audoen's Church.

Over time, the British established British law in Ireland, and although there were many rebellions against the British in Ireland, they maintained rule over Ireland until the uprising that took place over Easter week in 1916. During the Easter Rising, Irish rebels took hold of prominent buildings throughout Dublin, the most famous of which is the General Post Office (GPO) on O'Connell Street – the bullet holes of which can still be seen on the columns of this historic building.

Although this rebellion was quashed by the British, with many of those involved being jailed in Kilmainham Jail and many of the leadership executed, public opinion turned on the British, which led eventually to Anglo-Irish negotiations. The outcome of this was that 26 of the 32 counties of Ireland were to become an Irish Free State – a state that was allowed set their own laws and establish a police force, but whose Government had to pledge allegiance to the crown of the time in Britain.

The remaining six counties would remain under British law. This treaty between the Irish and the British, having been passed by the Dáil (the Irish Parliament), led to a civil war in Ireland in 1922, during which Dublin buildings such as the Custom House and the Four Courts were occupied and eventually gutted through bombing, destroying much historical documentation.

Ireland only became a full Republic in 1948, with the six counties in the north still remaining under British Law. The Republic of Ireland currently has a population of approximately 4.5 million, while there are around 1.8 million in Northern Ireland (some 6.3 million in total).

Dublin is rightly famous for the high proportion of poets, artists and musicians that have lived and worked there. Writers such as WB Yeats, Patrick Kavanagh, Brendan Behan, James Joyce and Oscar Wilde, artists such as Jack Yeats, actors like Brendan Gleeson, Colm Meeney and Colin Farrell and musicians such as Sinéad O'Connor, The Boomtown Rats (Bob Geldof's band), Rory Gallagher, Van Morrison, The Pogues (Shane McGowan's group) and, of course, U2 – all have lived in Dublin.

U2: the background

U2 – Ireland's biggest and best-known rock band – is a group still very much based in Dublin. The band is a four-piece, consisting of:

Bono	Vocals/Guitar
The Edge	Guitar/Piano/Vocals
Adam Clayton	Bass Guitar
Larry Mullen Jr.	Drums/Percussion

The members of the band came from four fairly different backgrounds.

Bono

Bono (Paul David Hewson) was born in the Rotunda Hospital in Dublin on 10 May 1960. His parents – Bobby and Iris – were from Dublin city centre – Bobby from Oxmantown Road and Iris from Cowper Street.

Bobby Hewson's father was a member of an amateur music-hall group based in the Father Matthew Hall, fostering a love of music in young Bobby. Iris was from a large family of eight children and, like Bobby, left school at 14. She had two sisters, Ruth and Sheila. (The famous Bewleys Cafe on Dublin's Grafton Street was one haunt where they would hang out, drinking coffee.)

Iris and Bobby were married on 19 August 1950 in St John the Baptist Church, Church Avenue, Drumcondra (Rev Fergus Day was the clergyman who married the couple), and they moved to a house at 36 Dale Road, Stillorgan, south Dublin. Bono's older brother, Norman, was born in 1952 while the family were living here. Eight years later, when Bono was eight weeks old, the family moved to 10 Cedarwood Road in the area of Ballymun on Dublin's northside. Bono attended Glasnevin National School before attending Mount Temple Comprehensive School, where he met the other members of what would become U2.

When Bono was 13 years old, in September 1974, his mother died of a brain haemorrhage quite suddenly – shortly after the funeral of her father. The effect of the loss of his mother at such a young age was reflected in a lot of U2's early work, especially in the lyrics of their albums *Boy* and *October*.

Bono's stage name derived from a hearing aid store on North Earl Street called Bonavox (Latin for 'good' or 'strong' voice). It was his school-friend Guggi who gave Bono this name whilst they were both part of an art group they called Lypton Village. Guggi still socialises with Bono, and the pair are occasionally seen together in the Coach House Pub in Ballinteer.

Bono is married to Alison Hewson (née Stewart). They met as teenagers in 1975 and were married on 21 August 1982 at All Saints Church, Raheny, with Adam Clayton acting as Bono's best man. They have four children: daughters Jordan (10 May 1989) and Memphis Eve (7 July 1991); and sons Elijah Bob Patricius Guggi Q (18 August 1999) and John Abraham (21 May 2001). Memphis Eve is now an actress, who portrayed the character Stella in the 2008 film *The 27 Club*. Bono lives in Killiney in south County Dublin with his family and shares a villa in Èze in the Alpes-Maritimes in the south of France with The Edge.

Bono is almost never seen in public without sunglasses. During a *Rolling Stone* interview he stated '[I have] very sensitive eyes to light. If somebody takes my photograph, I will see the flash for the rest of the day. My right eye swells up. I've a blockage there, so that my eyes go red a lot. So it's part vanity, it's part privacy and part sensitivity'.

Bob Hewson, Bono's father, died from cancer whilst U2 were on their Elevation tour on 21 August 2001: his death occurred just before U2's third performance at Earl's Court Arena in London, but Bono insisted the concert continue.

The Edge

The Edge (Dave Howell Evans) was born on 8th August 1961 at the Barking Maternity Hospital, Essex, in England to Welsh parents, Garvin and Gwenda Evans. With his younger sister Gillian (Gill) and old brother Richard (Dik), the young Dave and his parents moved to 10 St Margaret's Park, Malahide, on Dublin's northside when he was a year old. He attended St Andrew's National School, and later, Mount Temple Comprehensive School.

The Edge married his high-school girlfriend Aislinn O'Sullivan on 12 July 1983 in St Mary's Catholic Church, Enniskerry, Co. Wicklow, with Bono acting as best man. The couple had three daughters together: Hollie (4 July 1984), Arran (15 October 1985) and Blue Angel (26 June 1989). The couple separated in 1990, but were unable to get officially divorced because of Irish laws regarding divorce; divorce was legalised in 1995 and the couple were legally divorced in 1996.

During U2's Zoo TV tour (1992–1994), The Edge began dating Morleigh Steinberg, a professional dancer and choreographer employed by the band as a belly dancer for the tour's live performances. They became a couple in 1993, and had a daughter, Sian (7 October 1997), and a son, Levi (25 October 1999). They were married on 22 June 2002 in the Registry Office on Grand Canal Street.

The precise source of The Edge's nickname is unclear, but it's said to have been inspired initially by the sharp features of his face, but also applied by his sharp mind and the way he always observed things from the edge.

Adam Clayton

Adam Clayton was born on 13 March 1960 in Chinnor in Oxfordshire. The eldest child of Brian and Jo Clayton, Adam was five years old when his family moved from Oxfordshire to 7 Ard Na Mara, Malahide, on Dublin's northside, where Adam's brother Sebastian was born. Adam attended boarding school first at Castle Park School in Dalkey, then at St Columba's College in Rathfarnham. He later changed school to Mount Temple Comprehensive School in Dublin, where he met fellow bandmates Bono and Larry, and was reunited with his boyhood friend, The Edge. He took up the bass guitar and is entirely self-taught, although in 1995, after the Zoo TV Tour and *Zooropa* album, Adam headed to New York with Larry Mullen to receive some formal bass training.

During his long career with U2, Adam has occasionally hit the headlines for the wrong reasons. In August 1989 he was arrested in Dublin carrying a small amount of marijuana at the Blue Light Pub. However, he avoided conviction at Dundrum Court on 1st September 1989 by making a large donation to charity, and has later been regretful, saying 'It was my own fault. And I'm sure I was out of my head – emotionally apart from anything else. But it is serious because it is illegal.' Adam has also had alcohol problems, which came to a head on 26 November 1993 when he was so hungover that he was unable to play that night's show in Sydney. After that incident, however, he gave up the booze.

During the early 1990s, Adam dated and got engaged to British supermodel Naomi Campbell. He also had a long-standing relationship with Suzanne Smith, a former assistant to Paul McGuinness; they were engaged in 2006, but the pair broke up in February 2007.

According to the *Sunday Independent*, he fathered a son in 2010 (reported on 16 January 2011). The High Court ordered the assets of Clayton's former housekeeper and PA be frozen after it was reported that she misappropriated funds of 1.8 million. He married Mariana Teixeira De Carvalho, a Brazilian model, in 2013.

Adam's mother, Jo Clayton, died following a long battle with cancer on 9 August 2011. Adam's father still lives in the house they moved to in 2000 in Mayo. Adam currently lives in Danesmoate House at the foothills of the Dublin Mountains in Rathfarnham.

Larry Mullen

Larry Mullen, the middle child and only son of Larry and Maureen Mullen, was born 31 October 1961. He was raised on Dublin's northside at 60 Rosemount Avenue in Artane. Larry began drumming in 1970, at the age of nine, under the instruction of Irish drummer Joe Bonnie and, later, Bonnie's daughter Monica. His mother died in a car accident in November 1978, two years after U2 was founded.

Before founding U2, Larry was involved in a Dublin marching band called the Artane Boys Band (now known as the Artane Band). It was Larry who instigated U2 in 1976 by placing a now-famous notice on the Mount Temple Comprehensive School bulletin board, saying words to the effect of 'drummer seeks musicians to form band'. The band was originally known as the Larry Mullen

Band but the name quickly changed to Feedback, as that was one of the few musical terms they knew.

After U2 grew popular, and began making serious money, Larry added the Junior suffix to his name to stop confusion with his father (also Larry Mullen), who was receiving large tax bills meant for his son. Larry remains unmarried, but has lived with his girlfriend Ann Acheson for more than 30 years. They have three children, Aaron Elvis (4 October 1995), Ava (23 December 1998, named after the actress Ava Gardner), and Ezra (February 2001).

The band itself

In September 1976, Larry Mullen placed an ad seeking to form a band in his school – Mount Temple Comprehensive – from which he received responses from a few other students in the school, namely Adam Clayton, Paul Hewson (Bono), Dave Evans (The Edge) and his older brother, Dik Evans. Having had their first rehearsal in Larry Mullen's kitchen, they decided to call themselves Feedback. Two of Larry's friends, Ivan McCormick and Peter Martin, also joined in at this rehearsal. Martin didn't return after the first practice and McCormick lasted only a few weeks. Later that year, the band played their first gig in the school gym.

In 1977, they changed their name to The Hype. By March 1978, Dik Evans was being sidelined and eventually ceremoniously walked offstage at a gig in the Presbyterian Church Hall in Howth. The remaining four members finished the gig as a four piece under the name U2 (the name of an American spy plane), and the name stuck.

On 17 March 1978, the band won a talent show (the Harp Larger Contest) in the Stella Ballroom, Limerick, the prize being £500 plus studio time. (This venue is close to the Savoy Hotel on Henry Street, Limerick, where U2 played on 18 March 1978.) They recorded their first demo in studios called Keystone Studios (now The Harcourt Hotel) in April 1978.

This demo ultimately led to their first release, an Ireland-only three song EP called *Three* (aka *U23*), released in September 1979. The EP was recorded in Windmill Lane Studios, in June 1979. Produced by Chas de Whalley, it was released the following September.

The band recollect that Larry Mullen was studying for state exams that year and so his father would collect him from the studios. The process was that the drum lines would be laid down first, and the others would work on their parts once Larry had left. U2 also recorded a short studio session produced by Horslips' bassist Barry Devlin in this studio on 1 November 1978. After circulating for years in bootleg form, these songs were finally given an official release in 2004 as part of iTunes' *The Complete U2* digital pack.

The success of this EP led to a full contract being signed by the band in which they released their first album, *Boy*, in 1980, recorded in Windmill Lane again, between March and September 1980. It was a well-received album and Windmill Lane became U2's recording studio of choice right up to *Rattle and Hum* in 1988. *Achtung Baby*, although recorded mainly in Germany, was mixed at Windmill in 1991.

On 28 April 1978, Bill Graham wrote his first interview with U2 in the Irish music magazine, *Hot Press*. It was this journalist that introduced U2 to their manager, Paul McGuinness, and Graham maintained a good relationship with the band until his death in 1996. U2 appeared on many an occasion in this magazine and their first cover feature was on 26 October, 1979.

A DJ called Dave Fanning, who worked in pirate radio stations across Ireland in the 1970s, first gave U2 airplay. Fanning has always supported young, new Irish talent; he played new bands' demo tapes and gave them radio sessions. His very first session for the national broadcaster RTÉ Radio 2 (now RTÉ 2fm) was with U2. Indeed, his friendship with, and support for, the band, led to Dave Fanning's listeners actually getting to decide the A-side and B-sides of the band's first single release. The listeners picked 'Out of Control' as the first single, with 'Stories for Boys' and 'Boy/Girl' on the B-side. U2 once came into Fanning's show for five whole nights in one week.

In this period U2 were playing plenty of pubs and clubs around Dublin. The Project Arts Centre, on Essex Street East, is a live-music venue in the Temple Bar area where Paul McGuinness, U2's manager for most of their career, met with the band for the first time on 25 May 1978. U2 were supporting The Gamblers, and The Virgin Prunes opened the show that evening.

While McGuinness played a key part in U2's success, he was very nearly out on his ear at one point. On Grafton Street where there is a restaurant called Captain Americas. This was initially used as a meeting place for U2, and was where U2 were going to sack Paul McGuinness on one occasion in their very early days, until another manager, Louis Walsh (now manager of Boyzone and Jedward, among others), intervened. He convinced the young band to keep Paul McGuinness as their manager.

U2 were beginning to move beyond the small pubs and clubs, and picking up festival gigs. This won them a much-bigger fanbase. They played an open-air gig in Blackrock Park, Blackrock, Co. Dublin on 2 July 1978. With the release of U2's first album, *Boy*, in 1980, the band began almost endless touring, not only of Ireland but also the US. The band played the National (Boxing) Stadium on 26 February 1980: a venue that big-name musicians used to play in the 1970s, including the likes of Led Zeppelin.

In 1981, they played the annual gig in Slane Castle, Co. Meath on August 16, where they were the support act to Thin Lizzy. They returned in 1983 which marked the first indication of U2's real rise to fame. And the rest, as they say, is history...

Dublin

Dublin 2

POD ('Place of Dance')

The first of a number of U2-related locations on Harcourt Street is a club called the POD ('Place of Dance') where the single 'Hold Me, Thrill Me, Kiss Me, Kill Me' was launched on 1 June 1995. The club has had a chequered history of closing and re-opening.

Also at this venue, on 30 March 1995, during a Prince after-show gig, Bono joined Prince on stage for one song, singing 'The Cross' with him.

LOCATION: 35 Harcourt Street, Dublin 2

The POD nightclub on Harcourt Street, where Bono once joined Prince for an on-stage duet

The Harcourt Hotel: formerly Keystone Studios, where U2 recorded their first demo

U2 locations

Dublin 2
Keystone Studios

Beside POD is a hotel called the Harcourt Street Hotel, which was once Keystone Studios. U2 recorded their first ever demo at Keystone. In November 1978, the band performed a short studio session produced by Barry Devlin, bassist of folk-rock band Horslips. After circulating for years in bootleg form, these songs were finally given an official release in 2004 as part of iTunes' *The Complete U2* digital pack, which included the songs 'Street Mission', 'Shadows and Tall Trees' and 'The Fall'.
LOCATION: Harcourt Hotel, 60 Harcourt Street, Dublin 2

Dublin 2
Four Provinces/TV Club

Almost directly opposite the former Keystone Studios is a building in which the Irish Police Force (An Garda Síochána) currently has offices.

This was formally a ballroom called the Four Provinces, later to be renamed the TV Club (also called the Eamonn Andrews Studios), where U2 played on several occasions – most notably on the third leg of the Boy tour in December 1980. The only known songs from this gig are 'An Cat Dubh', and 'Into The Heart'.
LOCATION: Harcourt Street

Dublin 2
The Dandelion Market

Further down Harcourt Street, in the former car park of the St Stephens Green Shopping Centre, is where U2 played their earliest paid gigs in Dublin. The Dandelion (now a TGI Fridays) was established in 1970, a flea market where, for £6, a trader could rent a trestle table and sell anything legal. There were afternoon gigs organised there for young people who would otherwise have been prohibited, which greatly expanded U2's Dublin audience. Rory Egan of the *Irish Independent* (19 March 2006) told the Dandelion's story. 'In 1973, it moved to the former Taylor-Keith bottling plant in St Stephen's Green, where the shopping centre now stands. Using the old stables, mews and courtyard, the market doubled in size, with many of the stalls as permanent fixtures and most of it indoors. For six more years the market flourished. On May 12 1979, a young band called U2 played one of their first gigs in the courtyard.' The market itself had two entrances – one on St Stephen's Green and one round the corner on South King Street (almost opposite the Gaiety Theatre), with the market itself running behind a pub called Rices (now the main entrance to St Stephen's Green Shopping Centre.)

Known dates for U2's gigs at The Dandelion Market all fell in 1979, namely:

12th and 15 May 1979; 28 July 1979; 4 August 1979 Opening act was The Strougers
11 August 1979 An afternoon gig: U2 played Trinity College later that evening
9 September 1979; 15 September 1979 Opening act was The Scheme

9th Sept. 79 - U-2 play the Dandelion, a year to the day since their first step onto the local scene as support to The Stranglers at the Top Hat. The big, ugly crowd that roared for their blood at the start of their set were left at the end grudgingly accepting that the U-2 sound was here to stay.

What impressed about U-2 then remains the basis of their current appeal. Dave Edge's acid, offbeat guitar reminds one of Tom Verlaine; Edge is probably the best guitarist in the country. The band's trump card however is their lead vocalist Paul 'Bono' Hewson. As has been said before he is the most compelling frontman in the country since Geldof, with whom he shares an ability to draw a crowd into doing just what he wants. There are no "me artist - you bozo" affectations no pain-of-genius face pulling; he obviously enjoys himself too much. Added to the amphetamine puppet dances of this early stage act are new ideas and outlooks, including perhaps some garnered from his trip to London to watch The Master - Iggy Pop - at work (with whom he shares the habit of making up lyrics on stage) Adam Clayton is the solid, serious type laying down bass lines at the back. Drummer Larry Mullen is all flying sticks and schoolboy enthusiasm.

The group understand the difference between mere speed and real power. The set is varied in pace, the sound is now less cluttered, sharper, cleaner - but never sugar sweet. Through Bono is fed the band's energy. He is the focal point, the contact with the crowd. Clayton and Edge work unobtrusively to this formula. They never fail. The Dandelion is a big,cold, dirty venue, but up on stage there is no mistaking the presence of the big sound.

After the gig Larry and Paul are collared and dragged off to the nearest pub that will allow us in. Bono - paul - becomes affable, serious; the initial 'cool' facade is quickly dropped. We talk. How did they feel they had changed in the last year?

"We feel more in control. We let our real selves come through more, instead of forcing ourselves into moulds that don't suit us. We used to hype ourselves to a ridiculous degree. We're building ourselves up, holding out for a record deal that gives us what we want - total artistic control, allied with the marketing power of a big company. It's a high price, but we feel justified in asking it. We want to sell records. We want to be big. Independent labels are all very well, but mostly they preach to the converted. We don't want to be a cult."

U-2 steer clear of the incestuous self congratulation that sullies much of the undeniable achievements of the independent labels, They seek to transcend as many of the narrow tribal barriers within youth music as possible. Their music has many reference points to appeal to as many fans as possible. Let's just hope that

doesn't make their sound too bland. One U-2 fan, a member of another leading Dublin band sees their broad roots as indicating that "they don't know where they're at."

Teen life and it's attendent myths form the basis for their songs, songs cataloguing claustrophic frustration, self delusion, loneliness. They hate/fear the never ending process of myth fabrication in society. Altho they agree that adults too are made to feel inadequate by the non-stop barrage of advertising etc, they see teenagers as being the most vunerable to the process. "Books, movies, records all perpetrate the myth - it's great to be a teenager, Everybody's pretty/handsome. It's all Saturday night, disco, girls, coke. Everybody scores with everybody else. If this isn't happening to you, you feel abnormal. You get those mornings when you wake up and feel 'I'm ugly, I'll never get a girl - you become a victim of the myth. We want people to think for themselves, to see themselves as being as complete and as valid as anyone else. We feel qualified to talk about these things. We're still teenagers ourselves. It's all we've ever known.

Many songs catalogue the boxlike confines of most people's lives. The boxes are institutional mental; people surround themselves with self-delusion. "Birth, school job, marriage, death - it's all laid out for us. We can't escape, we don't want to escape. We say to ourselves 'this is all there is.' These are the kinds of themes that link the songs on our new EP together, and will do the same on our first album."

The myth-fabrication process manifested itself in a particularly vicious way for the group, at the Project the night before, beginning , while they were on stage with chants of "Paul is a prod!" - his mother is a protestant - and culminating in bottles being thrown at the stage. (great country this eh? No racism here pal.)

The 'street heroes' responsible were people from Paul's own road, "Middle class suburban kids like ourselves. 'Friends of mine. I can't understand it." Such myths are dangerous. 2 of the bastards responsible were later helping bouncers with their enquiries, ending up in hospital.

U-2 will succeed. U-2 will be stars. They will be big because they are good musicians, because Bono is a natural star, because they attempt to deal with the drab realities of teen life at a deeper level than say, Buzzcocks or Undertones. They are looking in on themselves, exorcising irrelevant myths coming to terms with the music and business ends of their profession. When this happens they will be formidable. On the other hand they might split up next week. Or stiff spectacularly.

Anyway, remember this for the present: if ears could talk, they'd ask for U-2!

Shane McElhatton

An early U2 live review and interview following a 1979 gig at the Dandelion, from *Imprint* fanzine

22 September 1979; 17 November 1979 Opening act was The Epidemix
23 December 1979 Opening act was The Threat
LOCATION: St Stephen's Green, Dublin 2

Dublin 2
Peter's Pub

In November 2015, U2 played four gigs in Dublin's 3 Arena, the first set of gigs by the band in their hometown for over six years. As part of the publicity surrounding the gigs, U2 were photographed at an old haunt: a small bar called Peter's Pub in Dublin's city centre.
LOCATION: William Street, Dublin 2

Dublin 2
The Little Museum of Dublin

Based in what was previously Solomon's Gallery on St. Stephen's Green, The Little Museum of Dublin displays three floors of historical exhibits related to Irish history

Above and below: a selection of the posters, album sleeves and memorabilia on display at the Little Museum of Dublin

throughout the ages. The ground-floor exhibition centre hosts regular exhibitions of Irish interest, such as exhibitions on the Abbey Theatre or Irish costumes used in the cinema, whereas the second and third floor host a more static Irish historical exhibition throughout history on a decade-by-decade basis. On the third floor is Europe's first, and most extensive, U2 exhibition. People associated closely with the band, such as Guggi and Paul McGuinness, contributed to the exhibition.

It collects old gig posters and photographs, a life-size Mr MacPhisto, signed albums, plus many collectibles. There is a recorded commentary (by Tom Dunne, DJ and former singer with the band Something Happens) as well as a bullet-point history of the band.

In December 2013, Bono and The Edge attended the exhibition, and signed the guestbook on their way out. The staff claim not to have seen or met either of them, with the

only indication that they were there being their names in the guestbook. The staff Christmas party was the evening before, and they claim they may have been too tired to notice.
LOCATION: St Stephen's Green, Dublin 2

Dublin 2
The Gaiety Theatre

On South Kings Street is The Gaiety Theatre, Dublin's main theatre. In U2's video, 'Sometimes You Can't Make it On Your Own', the end of the video was filmed backstage and on the stage of this theatre on 13 December 2004. The reason for this is that the song was written about Bono's father, who had cancer at the time of release of the single, and who used sing light opera at The Gaiety.
LOCATION: The Gaiety Theatre, South King Street, Dublin 2

A view from the stage at Dublin's leading theatre, The Gaiety

Dublin 2
Solomon Fine Art

Members of U2 visited this gallery on several occasions back when it was housed at 15 St Stephen's Green (now the location of The Little Museum of Dublin). Bono, Ali, and The Edge attended their friend Guggi's exhibition on 7 October 2002 – Guggi being a painter, sculptor and former member of the Virgin Prunes.

The Edge and Bono attended an exhibition by their friend Charlie Whisker, a painter and video-director (whose videos include work for U2 and Bob Dylan) here on 11 June 2003; and Bono and Ali attended another Whisker exhibition here on 18 January 2005.

During the summer of 2012, Solomon hosted an exhibition, sponsored by Jägermeister, of 32 rare early photographs of U2 by Patrick Brocklebank taken between 1978 and 1981.

LOCATION: Balfe St, Dublin 2

Guggi (left) and his former Virgin Prunes bandmate Gavin Friday, back in 1979. Nowadays, Guggi is a visual artist and Bono and The Edge frequently attend his gallery openings

Dublin 2
Captain Americas

On Grafton Street is a restaurant called Captain Americas. Similar in style to the Hard Rock Cafe, with many photographs and guitars hanging on the wall, it has been at this location since 1971. Captain Americas was used as a meeting place for U2, and was where the band were going to sack their manager Paul McGuinness on one occasion. Louis Walsh (manager of Boyzone and former *X Factor* judge), intervened, convincing the band to keep McGuinness with them.

On the 24 December 2009 and 2010, Bono busked on the street outside the restaurant. It became something of a tradition for him and in the following two years – on Christmas Eve 2011 and 2012 – he busked not too far away, under the archway entrance to St Stephen's Green itself.

LOCATION: 44 Grafton Street, Dublin 2

Captain Americas: the Grafton Street American bar and diner where U2's manager Paul McGuinness very nearly got the chop

Dublin 2
HMV

Bono signs vinyl copies of U2's *Rattle & Hum* album at a surprise appearance at a late-night HMV opening

More or less opposite Captain Americas is the music store HMV, which traditionally opened its doors the night before any new U2 album was officially released – thus ensuring all U2's Irish fans got their hands on the new U2 album first. On 17 January 2013, HMV went into receivership, and closed its doors seemingly for good; however, it has since reopened.
LOCATION: 65 Grafton Street, Dublin 2

Dublin 2
McGonagles

South Anne Street was home to the legendary live music venue called McGonagles, where U2's close friend, the rock journalist and broadcaster Dave Fanning, used to work as a DJ; a very young U2 gigged there back in the Seventies. McGonagles was known mainly as a punk and new wave venue during the late Seventies and Eighties, with bands such as The Clash and The Sex Pistols gigging there; it also had quite an active club scene. But it also hosted huge rock bands, such as Def Leppard in 1992. It is now, sadly, a shop called Smiles Orthopaedics. On Tuesday 19 December 1979, a now-legendary gig took place at McGonagles: the Hot Press Christmas party. The various musicians playing that night included: Fit Kilkenny and The Remoulds; Phil Lynott, Gary Moore, Scott Gorham and Brian Downey (Thin Lizzy); Steve Jones and Paul Cook (Sex Pistols); (Dave) George Sweeney and Paul Boyle (The Vipers); Bob Geldof and Gerry Cott (Boomtown Rats); Brush Shiels and, Noel Bridgeman (Skid Row), Phil Byrne (Revolver), and The Edge, Bono, Adam Clayton, and Larry Mullen.

The Christmas party, organised by the music and entertainment magazine *Hot Press*, featured impromptu performances by different musicians teaming up with each other. One such grouping was a Sex Pistols/U2/Vipers *ménage à trois.* Dave Sweeney of The Vipers explains:

'It was Paul Boyle [Vipers vocalist] ... who took the stage with Steve Jones [Sex Pistols], Larry Mullen and I ... What happened was that myself and Boyle were talking to [Paul] Cook and Jones who we had met in London on our tour with the Boomtown Rats. We were impatient for the live music to begin downstairs – the 'official' band for the Hot Press party were Fit Kilkenny and the Remoulds – so in true punk style we decided to take things into our own hands. We went below and without

> “In true punk style we decided to take things into our own hands. We went below and, without asking permission, we plugged in, Larry joining us ... with Steve Jones on guitar and vocals ... we crashed into ‘Pretty Vacant’ ”

DAVE SWEENEY (THE VIPERS)
ON THE U2/VIPERS/PISTOLS ‘SUPERGROUP’
WHO PLAYED AT MCGONAGLES

asking permission plugged in, Larry joining us just as we started. With Steve Jones on guitar and vocals, Boyle on guitar and myself on bass we crashed into 'Pretty Vacant'. We followed with 'Route 66' but at that stage we had gathered an audience from upstairs, one of whom decided to pull the plug on the supergroup mid-song. Back to the cheap wine we went...'

It was Thin Lizzy that had invited the Pistols members over to the bash. 'Phil Lynott was also at the party that night with Gary Moore who had just rejoined Lizzy and I remember an original Skid Row line up reunion with Gary, Phil, Brush Shiels and Noel Bridgeman much later in the night. It was Lynott who invited the two Pistols over; he was working with them in the Greedy Bastards line up and had just taped a spot on the Kenny Everett Christmas show.'

U2 played here mainly in 1978 and 1979, the 22 known dates being:

11 and 27 April 1978; 4, 11 and 18 May 1978 Opening act on all nights was The Vipers

23 and 24 July 1978 U2 opened for Advertising on both nights

30 and 31 July 1978; 2 August 1978 U2 opened for Heins and Revolvers

3 and 27 January 1979 The 27 January gig was an afternoon gig, for younger people to attend. U2 played in Trinity College, Dublin later that evening

3, 7, 14, 16, 21 and 28 June 1979 The 3 June gig was another afternoon gig for younger people

5 and 12 July 1979; 26 October and 2 November 1979 Opening act was The Blades

LOCATION: 27 South Anne Street, Dublin 2

Dublin 2
Kerlin Gallery

Just a few yards from McGonagles, on Anne's Lane, is the award-winning Kerlin contemporary art gallery. On 24 January 2013, Bono, Ali, The Edge and his wife Morleigh Steinberg attended a Guggi exhibition here.

LOCATION: Anne's Lane, South Anne Street, Dublin 2

Dublin 2

Bewleys

Bewleys' coffee is world renowned, and their coffee shop on Grafton Street is famous for artists, poets, playwrights and musicians over the ages to visit. Bob Geldof wrote the song 'Rat Trap', when he was in the Boomtown Rats, at this venue – rest assured that it wasn't a comment on the coffee shop's food hygiene standards. Bewleys was also the meeting place of choice for Bono's mother, Iris, when she used to meet her sisters for coffee in the city centre.

LOCATION: 78/79 Grafton Street, Dublin 2

Dublin 2

McDonalds: an unlikely spiritual Mecca

This, the first McDonalds in Ireland, was where in early 1978 Bono and a group of friends who had strong religious beliefs formed a prayer group after meeting a man named Dennis Sheedy. A customer had raised objections that Sheedy was reading a Bible in the restaurant – the precise reasoning behind their complaint being unclear. Once the commotion had settled down, Bono and the group introduced themselves to Sheedy and subsequently established a prayer group based around the notion that one should 'surrender their ego to God'. They named the group Shalom.

LOCATION: 10-11 Grafton Street, Dublin 2

Dublin 2

Lillie's Bordello

Lillie's Bordello is a well-established club that the likes of Bruce Springsteen and Prince have often frequented when in Dublin; it is also the venue where Bono celebrated his 40 birthday in 2001. Also, on 17 May 2003, Bono joined Tom Jones at this venue for a few drinks, after Tom played a gig in Dublin that evening.

LOCATION: Adam Court, 6 Grafton Street, Dublin 2

The after-hours destination of choice for rock's visiting aristocracy: Bruce Springsteen and Prince have both enjoyed a night or two at Lillie's Bordello

Dublin 2
Mr Pussy's Cafe De Luxe

Mr Pussy, aka female impersonator Alan Amsby

The short-lived Mr Pussy's was a cafe by day and a risqué cabaret-like hangout by night. Owned by Bono's brother, Norman Hewson, and more or less run by Gavin Friday, Mr. Pussy's makes an appearance in the animated video for U2's song 'Hold Me Thrill Me Kiss Me Kill Me'. Or at least, it did originally: the 'Mr Pussy's' sign on the storefront was deemed too provocative for the video and was re-drawn as 'Mr Swampy's'. Mr Pussy himself – a female impersonator named Alan Amsby – was the cafe's night-time host.

On the 14 September 1994, Bono purchased Charlie Chaplin's costume from Chaplin's 1940 film, The Great Dictator, for $53,400. This costume was framed and hung on the wall of Mr. Pussy's, alongside such kitsch items of memorabilia as a pair of Naomi Campbell's knickers. Pussy's hosted parties for musicians and celebrities including Van Morrison, Ronnie Wood, Christy Turlington, Mel Gibson and Michael Stipe. However, it was unsuccessful in its application for an alcohol license – booze had often been served discretely in teapots – it closed in 1995.

LOCATION: 21 Suffolk Street, Dublin 2

Dublin 2
The Old Storehouse Bar and Restaurant

The Old Storehouse Bar and Restaurant was formally called Eamonn Doran's, and is where, on 17 March 2000, Bono and The Edge performed an acoustic version of their song 'The Ground Beneath Her Feet' (with lyrics written by the novelist Salman Rushdie) as part of an interview by Chris Evans for the British TV programme *TFI Friday*. (This same session – a Dublin-based St Patrick's Day special – saw Chris Evans interview other notable Irish celebrities including The Corrs and actor James Nesbitt.) Radiohead played their first ever Irish gig at this location, back when it was named The Rock Garden, on 14 May 1993. It is opposite a restaurant

The Edge and Bono playing an acoustic version of 'The Ground Beneath Her Feet' live at Eamonn Doran's (The Old Storehouse) for TV's *TFI Friday*

called The Bad Ass Café where the singer Sinéad O'Connor worked as a waitress before her music career began.
LOCATION: Crown Alley, Temple Bar, Dublin 2

Dublin 2
STS Studios

Attached to a building fronted by a record store called Claddagh Records, STS was one of the recording studios used by U2 until its closure in January 1999, In 1986, Adam and Larry rehearsed here for what became 'Bullet the Blue Sky'. The song 'Desire' was recorded here in this studio in 1988.

The Edge fondly remembers the band's early days in STS Studios in *U2 by U2*. 'The first musical idea of real interest to come out of STS was a magic jam. I was playing around on a guitar part and Adam

Behind Claddagh is the former site of STS Studios, where U2 demoed material for both *The Joshua Tree* and *Achtung Baby* and Larry started playing along. At first I was thinking, 'What the fuck are they doing?' It was such a bizarre angle they were taking. I was almost going to stop the jam and get everybody back on track. Eventually we ended the take and I explained that they had been playing on the wrong beat, but when we listened back in the control room, it was absolutely brilliant. That was the beginning for 'Bullet the Blue Sky.'

It was also at this studio where the demos for what would be become 'Who's Gonna Ride Your Wild Horses', 'Until The End Of The World', 'Even Better Than The Real Thing' and 'Mysterious Ways' were recorded in 1990. In the documentary From The Sky Down (released as part of the 20 anniversary edition of *Achtung Baby* in 2011), STS studio appears in the footage of the band rehearsing.

Bono's vocals for his duet with Frank Sinatra, 'I've Got You Under My Skin' were recorded here in November 1994; the track appears as a B-side to U2's single 'Stay (So Far So Close)'. It was also at STS that, on 29 June 1992, Bono recorded 'I Can't Help Falling In Love With You'.

LOCATION: 2 Cecilia Street, Dublin 2

Dublin 2
The Wall of Fame

Located beside STS Studios, and part of the live music venue, the Temple Bar Music Centre, the side of a building here is adorned with painted images of great Irish musicians, such as Phil Lynott, Christy Moore, Sinéad O'Connor, Rory Gallagher and, of course, U2. DJ Dave Fanning oversaw the Wall of Fame's opening ceremony on 20 October 2005.

LOCATION: 2 Cecilia Street, Dublin 2

U2, Rory Gallagher, Sinead O'Connor, Phil Lynott and Van Morrison are among the many Irish musicians honoured on the Wall of Fame

Originally grey, the Wall of Fame has now been re-painted red

Dublin 2
The Irish Rock N Roll Museum Experience

Based in Temple Bar, and part of the studios and live venue complex known as the Button Factory, the Irish Rock N Roll Museum Experience offers tours of the studios and gig venue and exhibits about the musicians who used the venue – such as Sinead O'Connor, Thin Lizzy and David Bowie to name but a few.

Parts of the studios were used in the Oscar-winning film Once, and the studio where Thin Lizzy's Phil Lynott recorded his last sessions a few short months before he died in 1986 are also part of the tour. In the green room – an area of venues where the performers wait before they take stage – hosts not only photographs of musicians who performed at the place, but framed riders from some of the musicians – a rider being requests or requirements made of a venue by a performer – usually food and drink. There is a U2 exhibition of photographs and album covers in the gig area of this venue. One item of interest in this section is a jacket that was owned by Adam Clayton, who offered his jacket one rainy night to a woman waiting for a taxi. When she tried to give it back, once the taxi arrived, he told her to keep it.

Above: the Irish Rock N Roll Museum Experience. Below: U2's rider. Presumably all that booze was not just for the four of them...

U2 RIDER

24 bottles of rolling rock or a local domestic bottled beer
96 bottles of Heineken
1 Litre Cuervo Tequila
1 Litre Stoli or Absolut vodka
1 Litre Jack Daniels Black
2 litres Moët White Star Champagne
3 very good French white wines
3 very good French red Bordeaux's
2 Mouton Cadet red wines
2 Jacobs Creek or Black Opal Australian White Wine
1 Medium Port or Sherry i.e Sandeman

This book's author at the Irish Rock N Roll Museum, with a gold disc of Thin Lizzy's *Live and Dangerous*

Dublin 2

Hard Rock Café

This place has many items of interest to the U2 fan on display, including handwritten lyrics by Bono of one of their most moving songs, 'One', and one of the Trabants used on the Zoo TV Tour. Also on view here is a pair of Bono's blue-tinted sunglasses, which he wore in the 'Beautiful Day' video. Bono donated these glasses to the MTV 'Fight For Your Right' auction, which benefited Lifeboat, a non-profit organization dedicated to

Dublin's Hard Rock Café proudly displays a customized Trabant car from U2's Zoo TV tour

It was U2's guitarist The Edge who unveiled this tribute to Rory Gallagher in 2006

the prevention of AIDS.
LOCATION: 12 Fleet Street, Temple Bar, Dublin 2

Dublin 2
Rory Gallagher Corner

Irish guitarist and singer Rory Gallagher, who died on 14 June 1995, is remembered here – Rory Gallagher Corner features a copy of his guitar placed in the wall. The Edge officially unveiled this tribute to Ireland's blues-rock legend on 16 June 2006.
LOCATION: Temple Bar, Dublin 2

Dublin 2
Project Arts Centre

A live music venue in the Temple Bar area of Dublin, the Project Arts Centre is where manager Paul McGuinness met with U2 for the first time on 25 May 1978. U2 were supporting The Gamblers, and The Virgin Prunes opened the show

The Project Arts Centre

that evening. On 16 January 1979, U2 played at the Dark Space festival, a 24-hour event at this venue, with the band taking stage at 3.30am, winning them a highly favourable review from Dave Fanning in *Hot Press* magazine.

U2 locations

Back in 1979, U2 were merely one of 'Ten Dublin bands' at the Dark Space festival (left); and support act to The Gamblers (above)

Altogether, U2 played eight times at the Project Arts Centre:

17 March, 25 May 1978 and 18 September 1978

The September date was part of the New Wave Festival, an event that ran for about two weeks and which featured live music, film screenings and other activities. U2's gig was on the final night. The Virgin Prunes performed on the same evening, and Bono joined them for a couple songs.

16 January, 17 February, 7, 8 and 18 September 1979

The 7 and 8 September dates were two consecutive shows opening for Patrick Fitzgerald. On the first night, U2 got involved with a group of local punks who threaten to invade the stage. The punks were evicted, with Paul McGuinness dragging one out of the premises by the hair. On the second night, some of the audience were hostile, shouting 'Paul is a prod!' (i.e. Protestant) about Bono. Some bottles were thrown at the stage.

21 July 1980

U2 opened for The Blades: this was a 'secret' gig, U2 being listed as Feedback to keep their appearance as quiet as possible.

LOCATION: 39 Essex Street East, Temple Bar, Dublin 2

THE
CLARENCE
HOTEL

U2 perform a rooftop performance at Dublin's Clarence Hotel (owned by Bono and the Edge) in 1993

Dublin 2

The Clarence Hotel

The Clarence Hotel is a five -star hotel which was bought by Bono and The Edge in 1992.

The pair were for a long time struggling to extend the Clarence, but there were objections raised due to the historical nature of the buildings to the hotel's side. Permission was eventually granted, but works on the hotel were eventually shelved due to economic factors.

On 1 October 1993, U2 performed two songs (including a karaoke-style version of 'Daydream Believer' performed by The Edge) at the hotel during Gavin Friday's wedding reception (ex-Virgin Prunes singer and good U2 friend).

Another interesting feature of the Clarence in U2's history is that the promotional release video for U2's single 'Beautiful Day' was filmed on the hotel's roof on 27 September 2000. Views of Dublin, including the Ha'penny Bridge, can been seen in the video.

LOCATION: 6-8 Wellington Quay Dublin 2

Easons bookshop, where U2 hosted a *U2 By U2* signing event

The Edge, Bono and Larry Mullen, hard at work signing copies of *U2 By U2* at Easons

Dublin 1
Easons

Easons is one of the largest bookstores in Dublin. It hosts many book signings and launches, where many authors, musicians and performers have made guest appearances. The many notables who have appeared here include Graham Norton, Ozzy Osbourne, Peter Hook (New Order), Rafa Benitez, Pele and, of course, U2. On 23 September 2006, they attended a book signing event here for *U2 by U2*.
LOCATION: Easons Bookshop, 40 Lower O'Connell Street, Dublin 1

Dublin 1
The Savoy Cinema

The Savoy Cinema is where the premiere of the film *Rattle and Hum* was shown on 27 October 1988, at which U2 performed four songs – 'When Love Comes To Town', 'I Still Haven't Found What I'm Looking For', 'Angel of Harlem' (the first ever public performance of this song) and 'Stand By Me'. The Edge and his wife Morleigh Steinberg

The Savoy cinema, where Bono and The Edge attended the premiere of Spielberg's movie *Lincoln*. After the screening, an auction was held, where Bono donated some of the illustrations he had painted with his daughters (below) for his production of Prokofiev's *Peter and the Wolf* with Gavin Friday

and Bono and his wife Ali Hewson attended the premiere of the movie *Lincoln* here on 20 January 2013. At a charity reception in the Burlington Hotel afterwards, over £250,000 was raised for the Wicklow Hospice Foundation; the Edge bought signed scripts from the movie, while Bono had donated a set of the illustrations he had made for a book-and-CD production of Prokofiev's *Peter And The Wolf*, which were bought by Steven Spielberg's wife, Kate Capshaw, for £42,000.
LOCATION: 16–17 Upper O'Connell Street, Dublin 1

> **"U2 performed here as The Hype on 13 April 1977. At the time U2 were a five-piece band called 'The Hype' with Dik Evans (The Edge's elder brother) on rhythm guitar the fifth member. Dik later joined the Virgin Prunes"**

Dublin 1
Slack Alice's

Now a Carroll's Souvenir Shop, U2 performed here on 13 April 1977. At the time U2 were a five-piece band called The Hype with Dik Evans (The Edge's older brother) being the fifth member, playing rhythm guitar. Dik later joined the Virgin Prunes.
Alice's was located beside the Dublin Bus Offices on Upper O'Connell Street; the building had been rebuilt after the 1916 rising, initially as a chemist shop. The name of the chemist ('A and R Thwaites and Co.') can still be seen engraved over the door.
LOCATION: 57 O'Connell Street Upper, Dublin 1

Dublin 1
Bonavox

On North Earl Street there is a hearing aid store – if it's not the most famous in the world, it's certainly the most famous in Ireland. *Bona vox* literally means good, or strong, voice in Latin, and is the source of Bono's name. Bono originally wanted his name to be 'Bonavox of O'Connell Street' but was convinced – very sensibly – to shorten it to Bono by long-term friends Gavin Friday and Guggi of the Virgin Prunes.
LOCATION: Bonavox, 9 North Earl Street, Dublin 1

Dublin 1
Liberty Hall

Near the O'Connell Bridge, you will see Dublin's tallest building, Liberty Hall, on Eden Quay. U2 appeared at a benefit show for the Contraception Action Campaign here on 5 May 1979, which was protesting laws in Ireland that prohibited the sale of contraceptives.
LOCATION: Liberty Hall, Eden Quay, Dublin 1

Dublin's tallest building, Liberty Hall, on Eden Quay. U2 appeared at a benefit show for the Contraception Action Campaign here on 5 May 1979

The building on Windmill Lane where U2 recorded most of their Eighties albums, in all its graffiti-strewn glory

Dublin 2
Windmill Lane Studios

Further down the quays lies Windmill Lane, formerly the site of U2's most frequently used recording studio. The lane had previously been easily recognizable due to the immense amount of graffiti on the walls of all the buildings along it, making it a unique photo opportunity for visitors.

U2 recorded all their albums at Windmill Lane from their very first three-song EP, *Three* (also known as *U2 3*) up until the studio songs on *Rattle and Hum* in 1988. *Achtung Baby*, although recorded mainly in Germany, was mixed at Windmill Lane in 1991. The studio has kept the name, but moved to Ringsend Road, just outside Dublin's centre. Van Morrison is thought to currently own the studio, which have recorded the likes of Sinéad O'Connor, Kate Bush, The Spice Girls and The Rolling Stones in addition to U2. In fact, these studios were the venue of the notorious row between Keith Richards and Mick Jagger during the recording of the *Voodoo Lounge* album between November and December 1993.

The *Three* EP, which launched U2 upon the world, was recorded in June 1979. It was produced

U2's first release, the EP *Three* (above), was recorded at Windmill Lane. Sadly, little now remains of the demolished studio, its site awaiting redevelopment

by Chas de Whalley, and released on 1 September 1979. The boys recorded their *October* album here between July and August 1981.

Despite recording much of the material for *The Unforgettable Fire* in Slane Castle, Co. Meath, most of the album had to be re-recorded and completed at Windmill Lane Studios from 6 June to 7 August 1984. One of the last full rehearsal sessions for U2 at Windmill Lane was for *The Joshua Tree*: rehearsals and recording commenced on 1 August 1986. In January 1987, the B-sides 'Walk To the Water', 'Luminous Times (Hold on to Love)' and 'Spanish Eyes' were recorded here. It was during this period that the band fostered new friendships with musicians such

In 2000, some of the graffitied wall from Windmill Lane was sold off for charity, while other parts were given to Dublin's Irish Rock N Roll Museum Experience in Temple Bar. Today, not even the commemorative heritage plaque (below) remains

The Samuel Beckett Bridge, designed by architect Santiago Calatrava, is an impressive part of the view from U2's management's offices

as Bob Dylan, Van Morrison and Keith Richards and U2 started focusing on the roots of rock within their music. On 25 February 1995, Bono, The Edge and Irish folk singer, Christy Moore, recorded 'North and South of the River' at this studio, all three of them contributing to the songwriting. The song was released by Moore as a single.
LOCATION: Windmill Lane, Dublin 2

Dublin 2
Sir John Rogerson's Quay

Sir John Rogerson's Quay is where U2's management company, Principle Management, is based. Their office is in an old red-brick building, easily recognisable by the carved heads that overlook the front doors, which is on your right-hand side as you walk along the quays, lying at the foot of the impressive Samuel Beckett Bridge. It is a listed building (as are U2's studios on Hanover Quay) which means that, due to cultural or historical value, it cannot be demolished or structurally altered significantly.
LOCATION:
Principle Management are at 30/32 Sir John Rogerson's Quay Dublin 2

Dublin 1
The Point Depot

The O2 live music venue, formally known as The Point Depot, is located on the North

Wall Quay. U2 filmed two songs here – 'Van Diemans Land' and 'Desire' – in May 1988, as well as some interview material, for their film *Rattle and Hum*, and they subsequently played at The Point for four nights, culminating in their New Year's Eve gig in 1989 (the gig dates were 26, 27, 30 and 31 December). B.B. King was the opening act for this set of shows, returning to the stage at the end of the evening to duet with Bono on 'Love Rescue Me' and 'When Love Comes To Town'. It was during this set of gigs, U2 – tired and demoralised from long tours, having received ardent criticism of their film, *Rattle and Hum* – the band announced that they were going to 'get back in their box' and have to go and 'dream it all up again', fueling speculation that U2 were breaking up. In fact, they spent almost the subsequent following two years writing and recording *Achtung Baby* – a brand new direction for the band and one of their best-received albums. On 6 February 1993, Bono

The video for 'Pride (In the Name of Love)' was directed by Donald Cammell (a legendary director who filmed the cult movie *Performance*). The video features several aerial shots of Dublin's docks, whilst the East-Link toll bridge, opposite The Point/O2, is featured prominently

sung two songs at a Van Morrison concert at the Point. Frank Sinatra celebrated his 80th birthday in 1995, and as part of the celebrations, a TV programme was aired on 14 December 1995 featuring Bono and The Edge performing 'Two Shots Of Happy And One Shot Of Sad' – a song Bono had written with the intention of Sinatra to sing himself, but never did. Bono and The Edge's part was recorded at The Point Depot with a full orchestra.

In the late 2000s, The Point Depot was refurbished and was reopened as The O2. Bono and The Edge appeared at the venue on 27 December 2007, once again performing 'Van Diemans Land' and 'Desire' for the cameras just as they had done almost 20 years earlier. On 16 December 2011, Bono joined the singer Imelda May onstage here for two songs, one of the songs being – once again – 'Desire'. Opposite The O2, there is a toll bridge called the East-Link, which appears in the video for 'Pride (In The Name Of Love)'.

LOCATION: North Wall Quay, Dublin 1

Dublin 4

HQ (Hanover Quay)

HQ (short for Hanover Quay) is U2's current rehearsal and recording studio. As a (very) general rule of thumb, U2 have tended to work here, when in Dublin, from Mondays to Fridays between 2pm to 10pm, although they have been known to practice into the small hours of the morning. From 18 June to 26 July 1995, U2, Brian Eno and Howie B wrote and recorded the album *Original Soundtracks 1* under the band name Passengers at HQ. In January 1996, U2 started writing and recording what would become their *Pop* album here, as well as at Windmill Lane Studio and at The Works Studio. Apart from being U2's rehearsal and recording studio, this venue has been known to hold a few intimate U2 shows as well as a regular location

The Passengers' album, recorded at HQ, was a collaboration between U2, Brian Eno and Howie B

While the U2-related fans' graffiti outside HQ hasn't quite reached the same astonishing levels as it did outside Windmill Lane, it is certainly well on the way

for filming the band as part of documentaries and awards-ceremony speeches.

On 6 April 1999, U2 were filmed at HQ performing a few songs as part of a Johnny Cash tribute that was aired on TV in the US. On 16 February 2004, U2 played a mini-gig here for BBC Radio 1. Four years later, on the 25 February 2008, U2 were filmed at HQ accepting an award for Best Live Act from the *NME*. On 3 February 2009, BBC's *The Culture Show* filmed and interviewed U2 here for a documentary. In the film *It Might Get Loud* (2009), The Edge is filmed in Dublin in both Mount Temple Comprehensive School (where U2 met) and also in HQ Studios, where he is followed by the camera as he writes and records music. On 12 February 2009, three lucky fans were allowed into HQ. They were given a tour and treated to a mini-gig by the band.

LOCATION: Hanover Quay, Dublin 4

Dublin 2
U2 Tower

Benson Street is where the U2 Tower, a skyscraper that never happened, was to be located. This great lost project is sadly a boarded-up wasteland covering an area from Benson Street to the corner of Sir John Rogerson's Quay and Britain Quay.

The designs for the never-realised tower were announced on 12 October 2007, but plans were suspended indefinitely on 31 October 2008 due to the downturn in the Irish economy. Designed to reach a height of 130 metres, it would have been Dublin's tallest building; the plans included a pod at the top, which U2 were to have owned, as well as apartment dwellings below.

LOCATION: Benson Street, Dublin 2

It was to have been Ireland's tallest building: unfortunately the 'U2 Tower' never happened

Dublin 2

Trinity College

Trinity College is one of Dublin's oldest buildings. The current building dates back to the 1750s, but the original university was established on the site back in 1592. U2 played here on several occasions:

26 October 1978

An afternoon gig in Trinity College's Arts Building; U2 were playing in Bagnalls later that evening

27 January 1979

This gig took place in the College's Buttery. U2 had played at McGonagle's

WEDNESDAY 1 NOVEMBER
*Vipers (NW) UCD 1pm 40p
*Rule The Roost (R) Baggot Inn 8.30pm £1

THURSDAY 2
*Stagalee (R) Arts Block Trinity College, 1pm 30p
*The New Versions, U2, The Modern Heirs, The Virgin Prunes Arts Block, Trinity College. 7.30pm

THURSDAY 26
*Sonny Condell (Contemp) Coffee Kitchen 9pm
*Breton Folk Concert St Michael's Church (see Classical Music)
*U-2 (NW) Arts Building, TCD 1pm

Adam Clayton of U2

U2 played many times at Trinity College in the late Seventies (as can be seen by the gig listings above)

earlier that day
1 February 1979 The support act was D.C. Nein
28 May 1979 Stingrays and Fashion opened this gig, held in the Trinity Hall
11 August 1979 An evening gig, the band having played the Dandelion Market earlier that day

U2 were due to play at Trinity College on 18 November 1978, but due to the untimely death of Larry's mother in a car crash, the gig was cancelled.
LOCATION: College Green, Dublin 2

Dik Evans (The Edge's older brother), playing guitar for Gavin Friday in November 2011

Dublin 2
Leinster House

U2 attended a dinner here on 19 March 2004 in aid of the Irish Hospice Foundation. Reunions were had when The Edge joined his brother Dik on stage, along with Gavin Friday and Guggi, formally of the Virgin Prunes, to perform some of their songs.
LOCATION: 2 Kildare Street, Dublin 2

Dublin's Leinster House

Dublin 2

The Baggot Inn

The original live music venue that was the Baggot Inn closed on 19 August 1995 after 26 years, having hosted such legends as Thin Lizzy, David Bowie, The Rolling Stones, Tracy Chapman and, of course, U2. It soldiered on as a bar for another ten years but eventually became a Mexican bar/restaurant. Eddie Fitzgerald, one-time owner of the Baggot Inn, is fond of telling the story of how Bono was once barred from his own gig during U2's early years. The band were playing at the Baggot, they had finished setting up and Bono had left the venue temporarily. When he arrived back, the doormen refused him entry as he was underage. After much convincing, Bono was eventually allowed back inside the venue.

U2 played here mainly in 1979, known dates being:

U2 at the Baggot Inn in the summer of 1979 (probably 21 August). Over 2000 people in total saw them in just one week

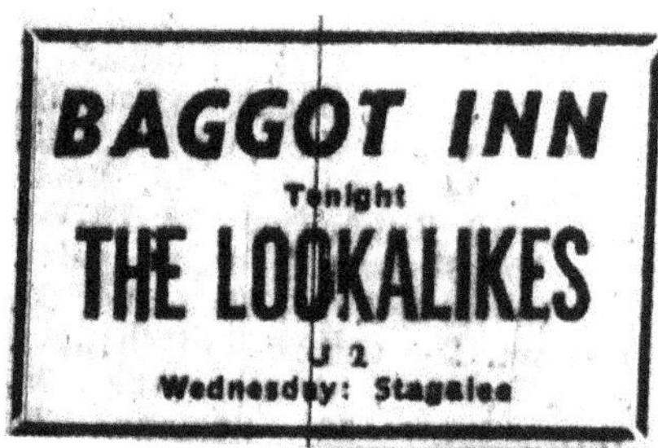
BAGGOT INN
Tonight
THE LOOKALIKES
U 2
Wednesday: Stagalee

BAGGOT INN
TONIGHT
U.2 WITH GUESTS
THE BLADES
Wednesday—STAGALEE

21 August 1979
Opening act was The Blades
17 September 1979;
24 September 1979;
2 October 1979

The 21 August 1979 gig at the Baggot featured DJ Dave Fanning and a band called The Blades in support. Fanning has saw U2 playing the Baggot several times during this period, and provides an interesting picture of the various bands around at the time, and their respective statures: 'U2 played four Tuesday nights at The Baggot Inn, supported by The Blades. I introduced the bands and was the DJ before and after the sets. U2 were on the up, but The Blades by then had a bunch of singles behind them, all of which I still regard as classic Irish singles. [The Blades'] Paul Cleary was a great singer

Bono says it with flowers in the video for 'Sweetest Thing': Fitzwilliam Square is pictured in the background

and songwriter, and they had a strong working-class following. But their live thrill didn't translate to their first album. At the Baggot gigs, though, there were still people who came for the The Blades and who left when U2 came on.'
LOCATION: 143 Lower Baggot Street, Dublin 2

Dublin 2
Fitzwilliam Square

Around the corner from The Baggot Inn is an area called Fitzwilliam Square. This is where the video for the song 'Sweetest Thing' was filmed in September, 1998. Amongst various performers that appear in the video are the Artane Boy's Band, which Larry Mullen was a member of when he was younger, and at the end of the video, Bono's brother and restaurateur, Norman Hewson, makes an appearance dressed as a chef. Shot in one take, it features a personal apology from Bono to his wife Ali, for having forgotten her birthday
LOCATION: Fitzwilliam Square, Dublin 2

Elsewhere around Dublin

Dublin 3

Croke Park Stadium

The national headquarters of the GAA (Gaelic Athletic Association) is Croke Park Stadium, Ireland's largest sporting arena. U2 have played here on several occasions:

June 29 1985 The Unforgettable Fire Tour: support acts were In Tua Nua, R.E.M., The Alarm, and Squeeze
27 June 1987 The Joshua Tree Tour: support acts were Light A Big Fire, The Dubliners, The Pogues and Lou Reed
28 June 1987 The Joshua Tree Tour: support acts were Christy Moore, The Pretenders, Lou Reed and The Hothouse Flowers
24 June 2005 Vertigo Tour: support acts were Snow Patrol and Radiators
25 June 2005 Vertigo Tour: support acts were Paddy Casey and The Thrills
27 June 2005 Vertigo Tour: support acts were Ash and The Brewery
24 July 2009 360° Tour – support acts were Glasvegas and Damien Dempsey
25 July 2009 360° Tour: support acts

A Croke Park date on U2's 360° tour

were Kaiser Chiefs and Republic of Loose
27 July 2009 360° Tour: support acts were Bell X1 and The Script

It was at this venue that Bono made a guest appearance at a Simple Minds concert on 28 June 1986, where he performed three songs with the Scottish band. On June 21 2003, U2 performed two songs here as part of the opening ceremony of the 11th Special Olympics World Summer Games, accompanied by a full orchestra. Nelson Mandela joined the band on stage during 'Pride (In The Name Of Love)'.
LOCATION: 3 Jones' Road, Dublin 3

Bono and The Edge, performing an acoustic duet of the folk standard 'The Auld Triangle' at Croke Park in 2009

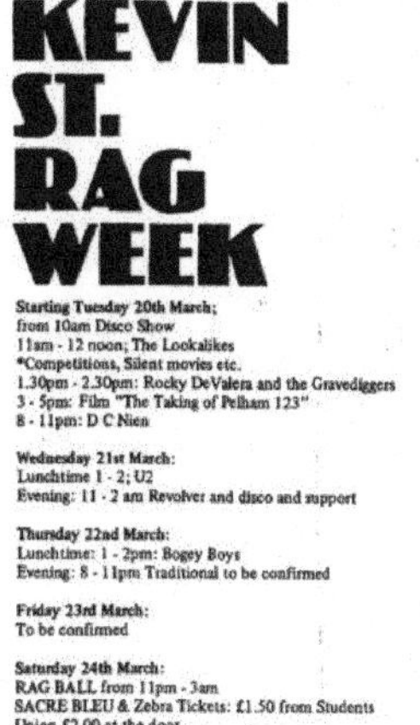

KEVIN ST. RAG WEEK

Starting Tuesday 20th March;
from 10am Disco Show
11am - 12 noon; The Lookalikes
*Competitions, Silent movies etc.
1.30pm - 2.30pm: Rocky DeValera and the Gravediggers
3 - 5pm: Film "The Taking of Pelham 123"
8 - 11pm: D C Nien

Wednesday 21st March:
Lunchtime 1 - 2; U2
Evening: 11 - 2 am Revolver and disco and support

Thursday 22nd March:
Lunchtime: 1 - 2pm: Bogey Boys
Evening: 8 - 11pm Traditional to be confirmed

Friday 23rd March:
To be confirmed

Saturday 24th March:
RAG BALL from 11pm - 3am
SACRE BLEU & Zebra Tickets: £1.50 from Students Union £2.00 at the door.

Dublin 1
Dublin Institute of Technology

U2 played a lunchtime gig here between 1pm and 2pm here as part of rag-week celebrations on 21 March 1979. Paul McGuinness, their manager, had made the band take a short break from playing live, in order to practice their songs and make the set tighter; this was their first gig after their chops-honing break.

It's also believed to be the first gig that The Edge used his now famous Flying V guitar, which he had purchased while on holiday in New York. Admission to this gig was £1.50 from the Student Union (or £2.00 at the door).
LOCATION: Bolton Street, Dublin 1

Dublin 2
The Olympia

Based on Dame Street, there are several associations between this venue and U2. On 11 February, 1993, Larry, The Edge and Bono joined Johnny Cash on stage with Kris Kristofferson. It was during this visit that Johnny Cash recorded his part for the song 'The Wanderer' for the U2 album *Zooropa*. The Edge attended a Radiohead gig here on 17 May 2003, and Bono attended an Alicia Keys gig here on 27 June 2004.
LOCATION: 72 Dame St, Dublin 2

The Olympia – where U2 duetted with Johnny Cash

Dublin 8
Christ Church Cathedral

This is a medieval Anglican Cathedral, mentioned by U2 in the song 'A Celebration' ('I believe in the bells of Christchurch'), and this is the centre spot where Dublin was founded. Some parts of the original boundary walls can be still seen behind and opposite St Auden's Church, nearby the cathedral.

LOCATION: Christ Church Cathedral, Christchurch Place, Dublin 8

U2's 1981 single 'A Celebration' referred to Christ Church Cathedral's bells

The sepia-tinted video for 'Pride (In the Name of Love)' (above) was shot inside The SFX. Below is pictured Westland Studios, where U2 rehearsed *Zooropa*

Dublin 1
The SFX

Located in Dublin's city centre, this is where the indoor part of the video for 'Pride (In The Name Of Love)' was filmed in August 1984. It was also the venue for a few pre-tour warm-up mini-gigs for the *War* album. This venue has since closed. The dates played were:

22 December 1982 Support act was The Big Thorp
23 December 1982 Support act was Zero 1
24 December 1982 Support act was Blue in Heaven
LOCATION: 23 Upper Sherrard Street, Dublin 1

Dublin 2
Westland Studios

This is a rehearsal and recording studio U2 used for rehearsing their material for their

The Factory: another of U2's *Zooropa* rehearsal spaces

1993 album *Zooropa*. Based on a lane just off Pearse Street, it is located beside the Wild Geese Martial Arts Centre. Westland was not the sole studio of choice for U2 at the time: they also used Windmill Lane Studios and The Factory Studios.
LOCATION: Magennis Place, Dublin 2

Dublin 4

The Factory

One of the rehearsal venues for U2 until Hanover Quay became their full time rehearsal and recording studio in 2000. This is one of the studios (the others included Windmill Lane Studios and Westland Studios) used to record their album, *Zooropa*. This studio has been closed since 2012.
LOCATION: 35a Barrow Street, Ringsend, Dublin 4

19th-century industrial architecture provided the ambience of the day at Adam Clayton's birthday party in 1987

U2 locations

Dublin 2

Boland's Mill

On 13 March 1987, Adam Clayton celebrated his 27th birthday at this warehouse complex, with over 300 guests in attendance. U2 performed 'People Get Ready' at the bash. Boland's Mill is located very near The Factory, and is on the opposite side of The Basin to U2's current studios at Hanover Quay.

The Mill's stone warehouse buildings date from the 1870s, while most of the rest of the complex are concrete silos from the 1940s and 1960s. Industrial production of one kind or another continued until 2001, but the building now stands derelict. It should not be confused with the nearby Boland's Biscuit Mills building on the corner of Grand Canal Street and Macken Street, which played an integral part of the 1916 Rising, and was occupied by Éamon de Valera, who would later be President of Ireland.

LOCATION: Grand Canal Dock, Dublin 2

Dublin 4

The Works Studio

Located not far from The Factory Studio, The Works was where part of the album *Pop* was recorded. The stadium on Lansdowne Road – Aviva Stadium, where U2 played dates on their PopMart Tour on 30 and 31 August 1997 – can be seen from here.

LOCATION: The Works Studio, 8 Grand Canal Street Upper, Dublin 4

The Aviva stadium, where U2 played during their PopMart tour

Dublin 2

Whelans

Based on Wexford Street, this long-established gig venue is a Dublin institution where the likes of Jeff Buckley, Nick Cave, Christy Moore, The Hothouse Flowers, and Peter Buck and Mike Mills from REM have all performed. In recent years, Whelans has hosted concerts for important new stars such as Damien Rice, Arctic Monkeys and the Magic Numbers. The Edge attended a Kelly Joe Phelps gig on 23 February 2002.

For an April Fool's Day prank in 2014, a U2 special intimate acoustic show was advertised for 'June 31st'. It even quoted Bono: 'It's been a while since we played Dublin. This gig is long overdue, so we're all excited and nervous, in a way. It will be fun, being an acoustic gig in a small venue so close to close to our hearts.' Mercifully, the webpage did end with a reminder that that day's date was 1 April.

LOCATION: Whelans, 25 Wexford Street, Dublin 2

Note the date of this supposed exclusive intimate Whelans show: an April fool's prank in 2014

The video for 'A Celebration' was shot in Kilmainham Jail, featuring the band both inside its corridors and outside in its grounds

Dublin 8
Kilmainham Jail

This is an old jail (the old English word 'gaol' is often given as its name), which is no longer functional; guided tours are given throughout the year. The prison has often used for film shoots (*Michael Collins* and *In The Name of the Father*, among others) and U2 used this place to film the video for their single 'A Celebration'.

LOCATION: Inchicore Road, Kilmainham, Dublin 8

The forbidding main entrance to Kilmainham Jail

Above: The Edge and Yoko Ono at the Irish Museum of Modern Art in 2004 attending Ono's 'In the Time of Shaking' exhibition. Below: the museum itself

Dublin 8

Irish Museum of Modern Art

In close proximity to Kilmainham Jail is the Irish Museum of Modern Art. There have been two U2-related appearances at this venue. On 3 February 2004, Bono launched an exhibition of Italian artist, Francesco Clemente, at this venue. In attendance at this opening were Gavin Friday, Guggi, and Paul McGuinness. On 6 May 2004, The Edge and Yoko Ono opened the 'In the Time of Shaking' exhibition at this venue.

LOCATION: Irish Museum of Modern Art, Royal Hospital, Kilmainham, Dublin 8

Dublin 8
National (Boxing) Stadium

This was a venue that big-name musicians used to play from the 1970s, among them Led Zeppelin, Thin Lizzy, and B.B. King. U2 played here on 26 February 1980, and it was after this gig that U2 signed their first contract with Island Records. In October 1986, U2 attended a B.B. King gig here and met up with him backstage. The band and B.B. King would go on to collaborate, writing and recording a song for their 1988 album, *Rattle and Hum*. Three years later, on 11 March 1989, Bono and The Edge joined B.B. King once more here to perform a version of that very song, 'When Love Comes To Town'.

U
2
Live
At
The
National
Stadium
February 26, 1980
Dublin, Ireland

A bootleg recording of U2's record-contract-winning 1980 gig

LOCATION: National Stadium, 8 South Circular Road, Dublin 8

Dublin 8
Tony Higgins' Studios

This studio is where Anton Corbijn completed a photo shoot for the album *Achtung Baby*, on 4 and 5 June 1991. It was from this series of shoots that the famous nude photograph of Adam Clayton was taken; which appeared on the cover of the same album. The Edge, Bono and Clayton commented on the nude photo in *U2 by U2*. Bono: 'The photograph began the legend that Adam is the most well-endowed member of U2 ... Some people think U2 should be hung. All I am saying is that we are, in fact, particularly well-hung.' The Edge: 'Adam is the most well-endowed member, no

Anton Corbijn's photos for *Achtung Baby* include one notorious shot of Adam Clayton in the nude (left, third from top)

contest, but he wouldn't know because he's blind.' Adam: 'This is indeed what legend would suggest, but I'd have to say that, within the U2 camp, I would definitely be the most diminutive of all the members.'
LOCATION: 33 Avenue Road, South Circular Road, Dublin 8

Dublin 15
Phoenix Park Race course

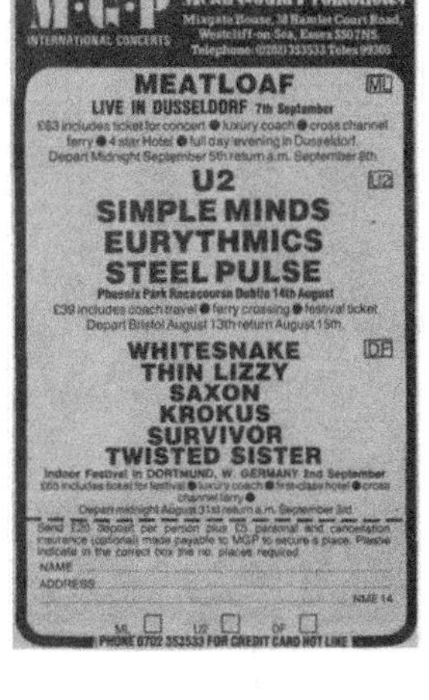

U2 played a gig here at the Free Peace Festival on 5 August 1978. This three-day festival had over 90 artists performing, including the likes of Clannad, Horslips, Paul Brady and De Dannan. U2 appeared here again as a headline act on 14 August 1983, when the Slane Castle annual gig relocated here for one year. Other acts at this gig included Perfect Crime, Steel Pulse, Big Country, Eurythmics and Simple

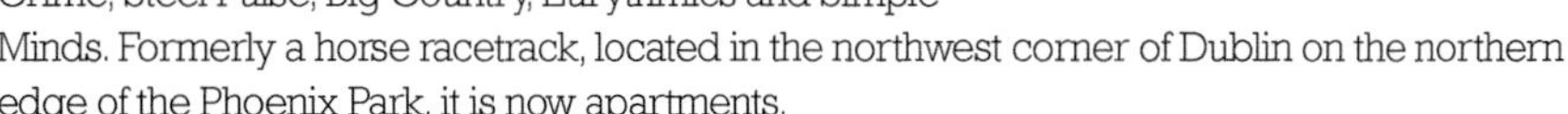

Minds. Formerly a horse racetrack, located in the northwest corner of Dublin on the northern edge of the Phoenix Park, it is now apartments.
LOCATION: Navan Road, Castleknock, Dublin 15

Dublin 2

Magnet Bar

This was a venue U2 played on several occasions. They first played here in September 1978 and again the following month. U2 also played a Rock Against Sexism concert at this venue on 28 August 1979. The venue is located opposite a hotel called The Pearse Hotel.
LOCATION: 130 Pearse Street, Dublin 2

Dublin 8
Mother Redcaps

This was the venue that hosted the Meteor Awards in February 1989, where U2 presented DJ Dave Fanning an award. Mother Redcaps is also associated itself with U2 as it is where, on 23 June 1989, Adam Clayton joined the singer Maria

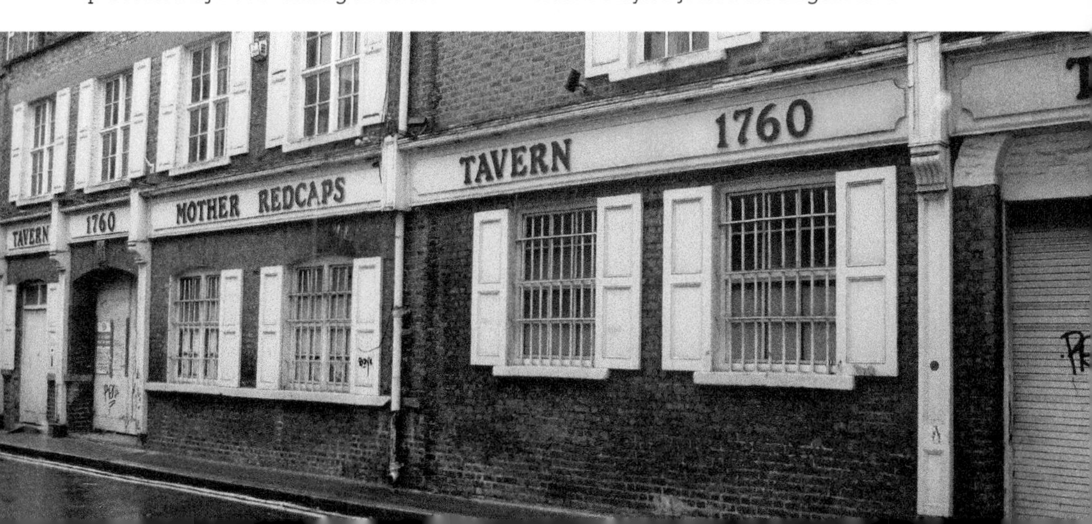

McKee on stage. This venue has since closed.
LOCATION: Christchurch Back Lane, Dublin 8

Northside of Dublin

Malahide

Malahide has a few main spots associated with U2, the principle two being Adam Clayton's childhood house at 7 Ard na Mara, and The Edge's childhood house at 10 St Margaret's Park. The Edge lived in this house for many years before moving Southside to Dalkey.

There is also a tower (converted to a house) overlooking the bay in Malahide called a Martello Tower. These Martello Towers are mainly found on the east coast of Ireland (concentrated mostly around Dublin Bay) and were built by the British as defensive forts in the 1800s. About fifty of these were built in total, and several people of note have resided in these over the years, most notably James Joyce, who lived in one such tower in southside Sandycove, which received mention in Joyce's book, *Ulysses*.

The Presbyterian Church in Malahide is the location from which The Edge's mother's funeral took place on 16 June 2012, and the funeral party retired to the Grand Hotel in Malahide after a cremation service took place at Glasnevin Cemetery.

This northside area has a rich association with U2. Not only does Larry Mullen currently live in the area, but it is also where U2 played their first gig as U2, in the Presbyterian Church Hall. They had played there several times before that, however, as The Hype on 17 December 1977, and on 4 March 1978. When they played here on 20 March 1978. Dik Evans left the stage half way through this gig, and the band continued the rest of the gig as a four-piece band, under their new name, U2.

The Presbyterian Church, where U2 played their first ever gig under the name U2

North of Dublin Bay

Howth

Howth was once home to a hotel called the Asgard, which merits a footnote in Irish rock history as it was owned by Phil Lynott (bassist and singer of Thin Lizzy) and his mother Philomena. But it also had a connection to U2. It eventually burnt down, and was replaced by apartments. Philomena recollected in her book *My Boy*: 'Bono later told me that his father Bobby had moved into the block of flats they built on the site.' Phil Lynott later bought his mother a house in the area, White Horses, near St Fintan's Graveyard, where he was buried after he died suddenly on 11 January 1986.

In the Howth area can also be found St Fintan's Secondary/High School where, on 11 April 1977, U2 played their first show in front of a paying audience – under the name Feedback. This was a three-act show, with two other bands – Rat Salad and the Arthur Phybes Band – also playing. U2 performed with two female backing singers – Stella

McCormick and Orla Dunne, who also played a flute during the show. Another place of interest in

The now-derelict St Fintan's Secondary School, where U2 performed, under the name Feedback

the area is the Community Centre, Howth in which U2 played some of the early gigs of their career, namely: 1 March 1978; 26 January 1979; 11 July 1979; 27 July 1979; 10 August 1979 (support acts were The Modulators and The Strougers); and 26 December 1979 (support acts were The Fast Skirts and Sounds Unreel).

Neil McCormick, lead singer with The Modulators, recalls the 10 August 1979 gig in some detail. 'We supported them [U2] again at Howth Community Centre in August. This was our territory, the hall was crammed and The Modulators played a blinder. Then U2 came on and ripped the roof off the place! They played a furious new wave rocker called 'Cartoon World' – written, so I gathered, by The Edge, which might account for why it had finished lyrics rather than relying on lots of 'oo-ee-oos'. Against a chunky, stop-start guitar, Bono delivered droll depictions of ordinary lives where the characters seemed to be increasingly dysfunctional, climaxing with the memorable couplet; 'Jack and Jill go up the hill/They pick some flowers and pop some pills!' With Bono roaring the punch line with maximum showmanship, hands aloft as The Edge's guitar kicked in the chorus, the crowd went absolutely wild. These were 'Beatles in the Cavern' experiences for me. I was getting used to seeing all the big names who came to Ireland, but U2's gigs were always the most special.'

Peter McCluskey of The Strougers also remembers gigging with U2 in Howth. 'We managed to blag a couple of gigs supporting U2. We had been to see a U2 concert at McGonagle's. After the show our bass player Shay Hiney, talked me into going upstairs to the dressing room to try and blag a gig supporting U2. Shay was the type of guy that could talk his way into anywhere for free. We went upstairs and burst into the dressing room, Paul McGuinness was sat in

Peter McCluskey, singer with The Strougers, at a U2 support gig, 1979

the corner dressed in a suit and smoking a big cigar. Shay informed the stunned Paul that we had just cut a demo and would like a slot supporting U2. Paul must have been impressed because we got our gig, we were to support U2 at Howth. It only dawned on us later: how do we get our equipment to Howth? We lived the other side of Dublin.

On the day, we had to take our guitars and drums on the bus to Dublin centre and then change buses to get out to Howth. When we arrived in Howth we had to carry our equipment up the hill to the Community Centre. When we arrived at the Centre U2 seemed very nervous, they did a long sound check, with Bono standing on the dance floor listening to the other to make sure the sound was just right, Bono was wearing his black-and-white checked trousers. The rumour was that an A&R man from CBS would be at the show – this could explain why Bono appeared to be nervous.'

LOCATION: Howth, Co. Dublin

Dublin 9
Bono's Childhood House

Based on the northside of Dublin, 20 Cedarwood Road is where Bono spent most of his childhood years. Bono lived here from when he was a few weeks old in 1960 until he was married in 1982. Located on the border between two northside areas of Dublin – Ballymun and Finglas – both areas have been referenced as the location of Bono's childhood house. In Samantha Libreri's book, *Finglas: A People's Portrait*, Bono explains the boundaries of the two different areas: 'There was a load of rows on Cedarwood Road about that very fact, because when we moved to Cedarwood Road everyone was saying we lived in Ballymun. Then at some point, I think when the seven towers were built and had built a reputation, some of the snobs around wanted to say 'No, no, no we're from Finglas'. So I asked my dad, who worked in the postal service, and he said, believe it or not, one part of the road is Ballymun and one part of the road is Finglas – so you can say what you like. Depending on whom we were getting a hiding off, we would say Finglas or Ballymun. I remember a terrible beating in Finglas, a big gang of boot boys, skinheads, running actually towards us and they stopped and they said 'Where are you from?', and I said [to myself] the best angle is to say Finglas, so I said 'Finglas' ... and they hammered us.' The book also features Bono discussing the practicalities

Ballymun or Finglas? Take your pick as to precisely where Bono's childhood home (above) lies

of his Catholic father bringing up two Church of Ireland (Protestant) sons in Finglas: 'We weren't really a big church-going family, but my father would drive my brother, if he'd agree to go, and me to St Canice's Church in Finglas, the little Church of Ireland church, and we would go to the service and he would wait outside or he would go over to the other St Canice's (the Catholic church) and get Mass and come back and be waiting for us outside. It seems to me so preposterous, I don't know why. It did then and even more so now. '

Bono recollects returning to Finglas shortly after U2 appeared for the first time on Irish television: 'The first time I did *The Late Late Show*, I came back and went to Superquinn in Finglas and I was mobbed for the first time. I'd love to tell you they were gorgeous teenage girls that were mobbing me, but it was a load of old dears who'd seen *The Late Late Show* and who wanted my autograph. '

LOCATION: 10 Cedarwood Road, Ballymun, Dublin 9

Dublin 5

Larry's Childhood House

Rosemount Avenue, Artane, is where Larry was brought up. It was in the kitchen of this house, no.60, that U2's first ever rehearsal took place.

LOCATION: 60 Rosemount Avenue Artane, Dublin 5

Dublin 5
All Saints Church & The Nucleus

This Church of Ireland (Anglican) Church, on the right-hand side as you come up from Fairview into Raheny, is known to many U2 fans as the Church where Bono married Ali Stewart, with Adam Clayton as best man, on 21 August 1982. Bono and Ali's wedding reception was held in the Sutton House Hotel (which subsequently became the Sutton Castle Hotel) in Sutton, a suburb of Dublin's northside, and is now a private residential estate called Sutton Castle. The church hall attached to All Saints Church also has a U2 connection: it's where the band played on 12 April 1977 and again on 1 December 1977 when it was a youth-club style venue called The Nucleus (back when U2 were still playing as The Hype).

According to a member of the Raheny Heritage Club: 'The Nucleus was the name of the youth club attached to All Saints' Parish in the Seventies. It was run by a members' committee, subject to the Select Vestry. I was a 'responsible adult' who was involved on the periphery for a period. The youth club met weekly with a different programme each week. They met in the old wooden Parish Hall (originally a sports pavilion from Saint Anne's estate). One of the regular features was a dance night with either records or a live band. The inside of the Hall at that time may have been painted black and the lighting consisted of coloured bulbs inside large tin cans.' As The Edge recalls in *U2 by U2*, 'We had a gig lined up at The Nucleus, a little club in Raheny, but we played so badly at the school disco that the DJ who worked at The Nucleus, who also was from Mount Temple, wouldn't put us on. He insisted on [us] coming to an audition. We played him

A happy day for Bono and Ali: the young couple were married at All Saints in 1982

some songs and very begrudgingly he put us on at The Nucleus.

'Before the show we decided to go and get drunk, because we knew that was what you did when you were in a rock band. So, as appalling as we normally were, we were just indescribably bad, and the sound was atrocious. We were in this tiny little prefab scout hut and we couldn't afford a proper PA. We recorded the show and a couple of days afterwards we listened to it in utter disbelief at what we were hearing. Bono was just bellowing and all you could hear was this really distorted noise that sounded like the early Stooges. Unfortunately I think we were playing an Eagles song. That was the same occasion when Bono introduced 'Jumping Jack Flash' and my brother (Dik Evans) started playing 'Brown Sugar', getting his Stones mixed up. It was truly one of the absolute low points. Everyone was out of time. On the recording you can hear the DJ leaning in when we we're halfway through the set saying 'Would you ever just stop? Please

stop! They're all sitting outside'. Listening back to that show, it was the first time I thought 'Oh God, no! This isn't going to work'. We were so hopelessly inconsistent. One show would have that moment of promise and coming together and the next three would be utter crap.'
LOCATION: 403 Howth Road Raheny Dublin 5

Dublin 3
Mount Temple Comprehensive School

This is the school that all four members of U2 attended. They met after Larry Mullen advertised for musicians on a school noticeboard.
U2 played here on several dates while they were schoolchildren:
1 October 1976 (as Feedback);
10 February 1978; 1 June 1978 (both 1978 dates were as The Hype; the support act was Frankie Corpse and the Undertakers).
The school also makes an appearance in the film *It Might Get Loud* (2009) where The Edge revisits the school and discusses his memories of the early days of U2.
LOCATION: 128 Malahide Road, Clontarf, Dublin 3

Where the four musicians of U2 first met

Dublin 9
Crofton Airport Hotel

Now called the Regency Airport Hotel, U2 played here in September 1978 to an audience of only six people. That didn't stop them being re-booked two months later, and they played here again in November.

In 1979, the band played here on four occasions: 2 and 10 January, and 17 and 24 June.
LOCATION: Swords Road, Drumcondra, Dublin 9

Dublin 16
Derrick Nelson Guitars

Nelson is U2's go-to guitar-repair guy and is located in Marley Park in Rathfarnham, not far from Adam's house. He has been repairing U2's basses and guitars since the late 1970s, as well as being a luthier who makes guitars in his own right. The Edge's technician/roadie Dallas School visits the premises on a regular basis to task Nelson with various guitar and bass repairs for the band. Nelson himself has been backstage at many U2 live performances and noted that Dallas School is not a man who leaves anything to chance: not only does he have spare guitars ready and waiting for The Edge, but also a complete duplicate set of guitar effects pedals.
LOCATION: Marley Park, Rathfarnham, Dublin 16

Adam Clayton liked writing and rehearsing here so much that he bought the place

Dublin 16
Adam's House

Based on the foothills of the Dublin Mountains in Rathfarnham, this house owned by Adam Clayton house backs onto St Columba's College – the school Adam attended before attending Mount Temple Comprehensive School, where he met the other members of U2. The house was initially rented by the band to write and record parts of *The Joshua Tree* album in 1986 and 1987, and Adam subsequently bought it.
LOCATION: Danesmoate House, Rathfarnham, Dublin 16

Derrick Nelson, U2's favourite guitar-repairer, hard at work for his client Ronnie Drew of The Dubliners

Two pubs that have very different associations with Adam Clayton: Johnnie Fox's (above), where he waxed lyrical about Irish traditional music for RTÉ; and The Blue Light (below), where he was arrested

Dublin 18

The Blue Light Pub

This is a pub located in the Dublin mountains, not far from Adam Clayton's current house, where Adam was arrested on 6 August 1989 for drug possession. He was subsequently ordered, in Dundrum Courthouse on 1 September 1989, to pay £25,000 to a women's refuge

LOCATION: Barnacullia, Sandyford, Dublin 18

Glencullen

Johnnie Fox's Pub

A pub in Dublin's mountains famous for its food and music. In 1990, Ireland's national broadcaster – RTÉ – filmed a programme on Irish traditional music there, in which Adam Clayton appeared, discussing his opinions and love of the genre.

LOCATION: Glencullen Road, Glencullen, Co. Dublin

Dalkey

Elsinore

This grand mansion-style house, found beside Loretto Abbey in Dalkey, is a building that U2 rented in early 1991 to finalise their writing of *Achtung Baby,* having spent some time previously in Berlin working on the album.

LOCATION: 7a Coliemore Road, Dalkey, Co. Dublin

Dalkey

Bono's Current House & The Queen's of Dalkey

Based in Dublin's coastline area of Killiney, Bono's house is located about ten minutes' walk from Killiney DART Station. The area borders that of Dalkey, where The Edge lives, as well as where The Queen's of Dalkey is located – a pub and restaurant that Bono is known to frequent on occasion.

LOCATION: Vico Road, Killiney, Co. Dublin; The Queen's of Dalkey, 12 Castle Street, Dalkey, Co. Dublin

Above: the main gates at the entrance to Bono's residence on Vico Road. Below: an aerial view. Left: in time-honoured tradition, another U2 address has received plenty of graffiti. Bottom left: The Queen's

Dalkey

Sorrento Cottage

Once The Edge's main home, the house known as Sorrento Cottage is found on a private road in Dalkey called Sorrento Terrace (at the end of Coliemore Road, where Elsinore is located).

Having built a small studio in his house, The Edge often recorded demos and parts of his songs at home; the most notable song to emerge from his basement being 'Night and Day', an adaptation of a Cole Porter classic produced by The Edge and Paul Barrett, which was recorded by the band in June 1990 for the AIDS awareness album *Red Hot and Blue*.

Sorrento Terrace is home to many notable celebrities. Neil Jordan, director of films such as *The Crying Game*, *Michael Collins*, and *The End Of The Affair* lives here.

Formula One racing driver Eddie Irvine also lives on the road, as does Van Morrison, while soul singer Lisa Stansfield lives nearby in Mount Henry on Torca Road, near Dalkey Quarry.

LOCATION: Sorrento Terrace, Dalkey, Co. Dublin

Dún Laoghaire

The Top Hat Ballroom

Located in Dún Laoghaire, south Dublin, this venue was famous in its day as it had a revolving stage, so as one band was finishing, the other band was coming on. U2 played here on 9 September 1978 when they supported The Stranglers. This was their biggest gig to date, paying them £50. Despite this, U2, and especially Bono, found this experience less than positive. In the book *U2 by U2*, the band described this gig in some detail.

'We landed the opening slot for The Stranglers at

Some might consider it a little large to be a 'cottage', but Sorrento Cottage is where The Edge recently lived, where he would demo ideas for U2 songs the Top Hat Ballroom,' explained The Edge. 'It was our first exposure to playing alongside a big band and a slightly disillusioning moment to realise that the punk ethos didn't extend to giving your support band a dressing-room or a few beers.' Adam recalls how the band were manager-less that night. 'Paul (McGuinness) had gone to a wedding. So he couldn't be our manager and fight for us. We had to make sure that we had a soundcheck and lights and a dressing-room, and that we were treated fairly and paid at the end of the gig. But I don't think we got a soundcheck, and they had taken all the dressing-rooms .... I know this was the root of what infuriated Bono later ... At the end of our set, Bono went into the Stranglers' dressing-room and got into an argument about heroes and how you treat people.'

Bono confirms it. 'I had a little argument with Jean-Jacques Burnel [The Stranglers' bassist]. I'm sure he'd never remember but it was a giant moment for me.'

On 14 November 1986, U2 attended a gig by The Damned here. The venue has since been demolished and replaced by apartments.

LOCATION: Longford Place, Dún Laoghaire, Co. Dublin

Dublin 4
RTÉ Studios

Based in Dublin's suburb of Donnybrook, RTÉ is Ireland's national television and radio broadcaster. As you might expect, U2 have appeared on many RTÉ broadcasts. U2's good friend Dave Fanning was a radio DJ for RTÉ's 2FM station, and U2 recorded many interviews with him over the years. Known dates include:

25 January 1982; 18 January 1985; 25 June 1987 In which both the band and Fanning apparently conducted the interview without any clothing; **5 February 2000; 22 and 29 October 2000; 11 June 2005, but aired on 22 and 23 June** An interview with Bono and The Edge for 2FM, held in Brussels the day after the Vertigo Tour opened in Dublin

The band's notable *Late Late Show* TV appearances include:

15 January 1980 The band performed 'Stories For Boys'

16 March 1987 U2 participated in the celebrations of the 25th anniversary of The Dubliners, performing 'Springhill Mining Disaster'

16 December 1988 U2 were interviewed at length and performed 'Merry Christmas'

18 December 1992 Adam appears on a special tribute show to Irish traditional musician Sharon Shannon, playing on stage with her on one of her songs

20 November 1998 U2 appear on *The Late Late Show* to perform two songs for a special show following a bombing in Omagh in the north of Ireland in the summer of 1998

21 May 1999 Irish TV personality Gay Byrne presented his last ever *Late Late Show* after 33 years. One of the highlights of the show was a surprise appearance by Bono and Larry, when they presented Byrne with his very own Harley Davidson motorcycle

31 October 2003 Bono, The Edge and

Their very first U2 appearance on the Irish TV institution that is *The Late Late Show*, performing 'Stories For Boys'

22 February 2008 U2 appeared on a Ronnie Drew (The Dubliners) special – and performed 'The Ballad of Ronnie Drew' with other musicians
29 May 2009 U2 performed 'Magnificent' on *The Late late Show* as part of Pat Kenny's last night presenting the show. The band presented Pat with a Les Paul guitar.

Daniel Lanois appear on a TV tribute to Irish film director, Jim Sheridan

Before they were even known as U2, the group appeared as The Hype on the show *Our Times* on 1 January 1978; and on RTÉ's Youthline on 2 March (playing 'Street Mission') and June 1978. Another notable early TV appearance witnessed them playing 'Life On A Distant Planet' on RTÉ's *Aspects of Rock* on 6 September 1979 and again on October 1979. On 30 January 1986, after a 30-minute interview with Bono and Larry on RTÉ's *TV Ga Ga*, U2 play two new songs, 'Trip Through Your Wires' (which eventually was released on *The Joshua Tree* album) and 'Womanfish' (which never surfaced again), as well as a rendition of 'Knockin' On Heaven's Door'.
LOCATION: RTÉ, Donnybrook, Dublin 4

Bono and Larry present Gay Byrne with a Harley Davidson motorbike

Dublin 4
The Burlington Hotel

Following the Dublin première of the film *Gangs of New York*, Bono and The Edge took to the stage with the house band at The Burlington and performed an acoustic version of 'All I Want Is You' and 'The Hands That Built America' at this venue on 9 January 2003.
LOCATION: Upper Leeson Street, Dublin 4

Dublin 4
Greg Carroll Locations

Greg Carroll, a New Zealand native, was one of U2's roadies up until the mid-1980s, and became close friends with Bono. His untimely death on 3 July 1986 at the age of 26, following a motorcycle accident in Dublin, led to U2 writing the song 'One Tree Hill', which appeared on *The Joshua Tree* – an album which was also dedicated to Carroll. Bono, Ali and Larry attended his funeral in New Zealand on 10 July 1986. The two spots in Dublin associated with Greg Carroll are close to each other on the south side of Dublin, and are within walking distance of each other, namely: Fitzwilliam Court on Wilton Road, where Greg lived while in Dublin; and the Hampton Hotel (then called the Sachs Hotel) on Morehampton Road. It was at the entrance to this hotel, early in the morning of 3 July 1986, that Carroll's tragic accident occurred.
LOCATIONS: Fitzwilliam Court, Wilton Road, Dublin 6; The Hampton Hotel, Morehampton Road, Dublin 4

The Royal Dublin Society (RDS), where U2 have played many times, and where they have joined the likes of Bob Dylan and Bryan Ferry as guests

Dublin 4

The Royal Dublin Society

Located in Ballsbride, this equestrian arena has been used on many occasions for live music concerts – hosting such musical luminaries as Bruce Springsteen and Paul McCartney. One of U2's earliest gigs here was on 14 June 1980, when they played the International Festival of Music. On 17 May 1986, U2 performed as part of the Self Aid concert at this venue. The Edge joined Bryan Ferry on stage here in November 1988. This is also where Bono joined Bob Dylan on stage at this venue on 4 June 1989.
U2 played the Irish leg of the October Tour on 26 January 1982, and again for the Zoo TV Tour – aka the Zooropa Tour, as it was renamed when it came to Europe – on 27 and 28 August 1993. Marxman and The Golden Horde supported the band on the first night, with Scary Éire and Stereo MCs supporting them on the second night. On the second of the two nights of the Zooropa Tour in Dublin, Naomi Campbell – Adam's fiancée at the time – appeared on stage
LOCATION: Ballsbridge, Dublin 4

Dublin 18

Spruce Avenue

This location is where the indoor part of the video for U2's 'The Fly' was recorded on 13 September 1991. At the time, the premises at which the video was filmed was Film Lighting Facilities, which has since closed.

The video for 'The Fly' was shot inside a location at Spruce Avenue

The video itself was directed by Ritchie Smyth and Jon Klein (founder of Batcave, former member of Specimen and later guitarist for Siouxsie and the Banshees). Ritchie Smyth subsequently directed various other U2 videos, including 'Until The End Of The World' and 'Last Night On Earth'.
LOCATION: Spruce Avenue, Sandyford, Dublin 18

Kildare

Leixlip Castle (above), where U2 played their first open-air festival; Adam (right) is seen performing '11 'O Clock Tick Tock' at that gig

Leixlip

Leixlip Castle

This venue hosted a U2 gig on 27 July 1980. This was U2's first open-air festival, to an audience of 15,000. The Police headlined the festival, with other bands on the bill including Squeeze and Q-Tips.

LOCATION: Main Street, Leixlip, Co. Kildare

Ballymore Eustace
Barretstown Castle

On 4 September, 2004, The Edge performed a duet with Paul McCartney at a fundraiser in aid of the 10th anniversary of children's charity Barretstown, a charity that provides a camp for children with serious illnesses.
LOCATION: Ballymore Eustace, Co. Kildare

Punchestown
Punchestown Racecourse

U2 played at this venue on 18 July 1982. This was a celebration of *Hot Press* being in existence for five years. Bono brought Ali on stage during this gig.
LOCATION: Punchestown, Naas, Co. Kildare

Meath

Slane

Slane Castle

Based in County Meath, and about an hour's drive from Dublin City Centre, this castle is probably most famous for its annual gig, hosting many major artists play. Bands such as the Red Hot Chili Peppers, Bruce Springsteen, Robbie Williams, Guns and Roses, as well as U2, all have headlined here. In fact, U2 played here for the first time on 16 August 1981 when they were supporting Thin Lizzy. The Slane Castle gig was held in the Phoenix Park Racecourse on 14 August 1983, when U2 headlined. They subsequently were the only band to play here twice in one year in 2001 (25 August and 1 September 2001).

The 2001 gigs were especially poignant as Bob Hewson, Bono's father, died less than a week beforehand, but Bono insisted that the show must continue. The two nights of this show in 2001 were caught on a DVD entitled *U2 Go Home*. The support acts for the two 2001 gigs were as follows: 25 August 2001 (Relish, JJ72, Kelis, Coldplay, and Red Hot Chili Peppers); 1 September 2001 (Ash, Moby, Nelly Furtado, The Walls, and Dara. The Foo Fighters had planned to play at this gig, but their slot was cancelled). Bono joined Bob Dylan on stage

The Edge and Bono at a U2 gig in the grounds of Slane Castle, 2001

here on 8 July 1984. Alex Mountcharles, son of the owner of Slane Castle, Henry Mountcharles, recollects U2 visiting the castle for the *Unforgettable Fire* recordings, and remembers sneaking down to look at the instruments left out for the next day's recordings. He also remembers Bono playing 'ambulance' with the children of the house. U2 have a close relationship with the owners of the Castle, instigated by Paul McGuinness who had done some early film work there. So close is the relationship between the Montcharles family and the group that Adam Clayton is the godfather of Henry Montcharles' daughter, Henrietta Conynham.

LOCATION: Slane Castle, Slane, Co. Meath

Westmeath

Moydrum

Moydrum Castle

Based in Westmeath, and about 90 minutes from Dublin City Centre, this is the castle that appears on the cover of *The Unforgettable Fire* album. It is quite difficult to locate, and is probably best reached by car, heading on the main Dublin to Galway road, and there is a turn off just before you reach Athlone.

LOCATION: Moydrum, Co. Westmeath

Mullingar

Bagnalls

U2 played here on 26 October 1978, their second gig of the day having played at Trinity College, Dublin (TCD) earlier that afternoon. They were advertised as 'The U2 Band' for this gig. Bagnalls was located off the main Dublin-to-Galway road, situated beside a convenience store called Centre.

LOCATION: Dublin Road, Rochfortbridge, Mullingar, Co. Westmeath

More from the Moydrum Castle sessions (above) and a typical view of the castle itself (top right). Below: Bagnalls

Limerick

Limerick City

The Crescent Hall

U2 played at the Crescent Hall (situated on The Crescent in Limerick city centre) on 21 February 1980. The support act was The Kidz, as part of a tour promoting their second single, 'Another Day'. This venue was attached to the Jesuit Church, and issues arising from the Crescent Hall gig led to a NIHE gig, due to be played on 15 May 1980, being cancelled. According to Ber Angley, the Entertainments Officer at NIHE/UL for many years, who was involved in this gig, along with the late Brendan Murray, who was the main concert promoter in Limerick and manager of The Savoy Theatre,, there was a disappointing crowd of only about 200 at the show. Some time after the gig at the Crescent Hall, Bono was very critical of the Limerick audience in an interview. As a consequence Angley refused to book them for gigs at NIHE, so they never played at the university.

According to Mike Maguire, a friend of Ber's: 'As I recall it, Bono had cause to be critical – for one song Bono brought a

Right: poster for U2's tour in early 1980.
Below: the entrance to the Crescent Hall

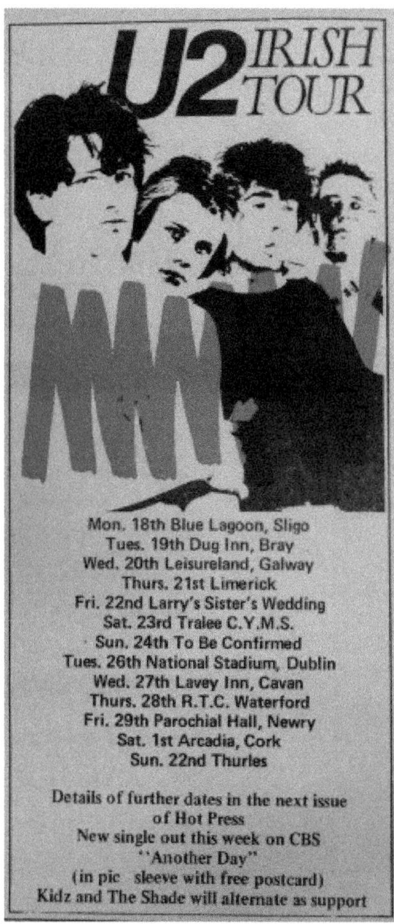

floor-tom drum centre-stage and gestured to the audience for someone to come up. Before I even registered what was happening, my friend, Ger Benson was on the stage and Bono handed him drum sticks and gestured for him to play along with the song the band were playing. Then a prime specimen of Limerick thug jumped on stage, grabbed the sticks off Ger and pushed him away. Ger appealed to Bono who, probably wisely, refused to get involved! Ger came off the stage very disgruntled and got beaten up later on for his trouble! I believe there was a good bit of trouble at the gig although I didn't witness any of it as I was right at the front. A friend of mine, Eoin Devereux, was a DJ on one of the pirate radio stations at the time and he interviewed Bono after the gig and he said that Bono was very unhappy with the crowd's behaviour and said it was unlikely the band would play in Limerick again.' According to Ber himself, 'U2 Never played NIHE. I was involved with the show at the Crescent Theatre in Limerick with local promoter, Brendan Murray, RIP. From what I gather, there was only just over 200 at the gig. I did refuse them a gig at the NIHE – I was very young and inexperienced at the time. I was with Brendan when we booked the venue from the priest in charge: Brendan called them a modern folk band - the priest was a little shocked when U2 took to the stage.'
LOCATION: The Crescent, Limerick City

Cork

Cork City

Cork Opera House

The opera house was a venue U2 played on 5 October 1979. They played here again on 23 October of the same year when the gig was televised by the Irish national broadcaster, RTÉ, giving U2 one of their earliest television performances. U2 opened for the band Horslips on this occasion.
LOCATION: Emmet Place, Cork City

Cork Opera House, as it is today

Above left: a 1979 events programme for Cork Opera House. Above right: the not exactly Arcadian-looking Arcadia Hall, where The Arcadia once stood

Cork City
The Arcadia

This old venue (now student accommodation) was located opposite Cork's main train station. U2 played here on several occasions in their early days, namely:

23 September 1978 U2 open for D.C. Nien
30 September 1978 U2 open for XTC
1 October 1978
26 May 1979 U2 open for The Only Ones
1 September 1979 U2 open for D.C. Nien
3 November 1979 U2 open for The Tearjerkers
24 November 1979 U2 open for Nun Attax
29 December 1979 U2 open for Protex
17 May 1980 U2 open for Mystery Men
20 December 1980 U2 open for Microdisney
LOCATION: Lower Glanmie Road, Cork

Cork City
Páirc Ui Chaoimh

U2 played here as part of their *Joshua Tree* Tour on 8 August 1987 (support acts were The Dubliners, UB40, and The Subterraneans), and again as part of their Zoo TV Tour, on 24 August 1993 (support acts were Engine Alley and Utah Saints).

LOCATION: Ballintemple, Cork City, Co. Cork

Cork City Country Club

U2 played here on 4 February 1980. It was also the venue whose rooftop views over the city ended up on the album cover *U218*, released on 20 November 2006. The photographer who took this famous shot, David Corio, admits he had never heard of U2 when he took the photo.
LOCATION: Montenotte, Cork City, Co. Cork

The cover of *U218* uses a photo of the band taken on the rooftop of the Montenotte Country Club in Cork City

Cork City Lark by The Lee

U2 played here on 25 August 1985. This festival was held on the Lee Fields area on the Carrigrohane Road in central Cork city. The site backs onto an area where a recently closed-down Kingsley Hotel is located. U2 weren't officially billed for the gig in 1985, but played a surprise set after the local bands had finished.
LOCATION: Lee Fields, Carrigrohane Road, Cork City

84 The Stardust

U2 played here on 11 December 1978, as support to The Greedy Bastards, a band made up of members of the Sex Pistols and Thin Lizzy. They played here again on 7 July 1979. This venue subsequently became the Grand Parade

The Stardust is now demolished, its site boarded-up

Hotel, which has since closed. The same complex used to house the club Sir Henrys, where Nirvana supported Sonic Youth in the early 1990s.
LOCATION: 66 Grand Parade, Greenmount, Cork City

Dennehy's Cross
St Oliver's Cemetery

Rory Gallagher, one of The Edge's musical inspirations, died on 14 June 1995 following complications from a liver transplant. He was buried at this graveyard on 19 June 1995, following his funeral mass at the Church of the Holy Ghost (also known as the Church of the Holy Spirit) located at Dennehys Cross, Cork. In attendance were many musicians including Ronnie Drew of the Dubliners (who spoke from the Book of Wisdom at the funeral), blues guitarist, Gary Moore, as well as Adam Clayton and The Edge. The sunray design of the gravestone is based on one of Rory Gallagher's awards – the International Guitarist of the Year in 1972.

Rory Gallagher's grave at St Oliver's Cemetery

LOCATION: Church of the Holy Ghost, Dennehy's Cross, Cork

Cork City
Jackie Lennox Chipper

This fish and chip shop – established over 60 years ago – has its connection with U2 when, in 1985, the owner bid for, and won, a U2 War Gold Disc as part of a Live Aid auction. Bono himself presented the disc to the owner.
LOCATION: 137 Bandon Road, Cork

Waterford

The Glen
The Showboat

SHOWBOAT
THURSDAY, MAY 8th
SIMON
FRIDAY
SONUS
(Top 7 Piece Traditional Group)
SATURDAY
NIGHTBUS
SUNDAY
DROPS OF BRANDY
MONDAY, MAY 12th
Showboat Soccer Club — starring
SIMON, WAVES
LEO WALSH
DASHER BOLGER
AND MANY MORE
TUESDAY 13th MAY
WATERFORD ROSE OF TRALEE ENTRANT
TO BE CHOSEN. Music by
PARTNERS
Plus Carling Black Label £1,000 Talent Competition
Also Friendly Fortune. £100 to be won each night
WEDNESDAY
U TWO
(Voted Ireland's Top Rock Band in 1979)
THURSDAY 15th MAY
SIMON

U2 played here on 14 May 1980, with the band Myster Men, as support act. U2 opened their set with their new single, '11 O'clock Tick Tock' on this particular tour. Frank Kearns, guitarist with the Myster Men, was also at Mount Temple Comprehensive School with U2, and was a friend of Larry's.

The Myster Men recorded a three-track demo that was produced by Bono, who also sang backing vocals, the tracks being: 'No More Idols', 'Fantasy Dream' and 'I Should Have Known Better'. Eric Briggs, drummer with the Myster Men, was U2's drum technician from 1978 to 1980, according to *U2 by U2*. He also stood in at rehearsals for Larry when Larry could not make it due to his day job. At one point,

Bono was talking of Eric being the permanent drummer with U2, although Eric never stood in for Larry at a concert.

The Myster Men were tipped as the next big thing by *Zig Zag* magazine. U2 are incorrectly listed as 'U Two' in the local press.

LOCATION: 18 The Glen, Waterford, Kerry

Wicklow

Bray
Ardmore Studios

These studios, part-owned by Paul McGuinness, and based in Bray, Co. Wicklow, is where Bono joined Irish band, The Corrs, onstage for two songs in a performance taped by VH1 on 25 January 2002. Also, in February 1987, the video for 'With Or Without You' was filmed here. Many well-known films have been shot at these studios such as *Braveheart* and *My Left Foot*, as well as TV series such as *The Tudors*.

LOCATION: Herbert Road, Bray, Co. Wicklow

Bray
Martello Tower

In the 1980s, Bono owned this historical building on the coast of the Irish Sea, before moving to his house in Killiney. Bono describes here in *U2 by U2*:

'It's an extraordinary place to live. And the band even rehearsed there. We worked up some of the songs there: 'Pride', 'Unforgettable Fire', 'A Sort of Homecoming.''

LOCATION: Strand Road, Bray, Co. Wicklow, Wexford

Gorey

Gorey Theatre Hall

U2 headlined the 11 Gorey Arts Festival on 15 August 1980. The Virgin Prunes had headlined the same festival in 1979. This Festival ran between 1970 and 1984, and was subsequently revived as the Gorey Arts and Film Festival.

LOCATION: Gorey Town Council, Civic Square, The Avenue, Gorey, Co. Wexford

Gorey Arts Festival

BOOKING
ARTS CENTRE
055 — 21470.

Thursday 9pm	TREASA O'DRISCOLL and MICHAEL O'DOMHNAILL.
Friday 3.30pm	SUNFLOWER presented by TEAM.
Friday 9pm	JOHN O'CONOR and VERONICA DUNNE, an evening of classical music.
Saturday 9pm	LOUIS STEWART, jazz guitarist.
Sunday 9pm	ANNE BUSHNELL with 15 piece jazz orchestra.
Monday 9pm	MAKEM & CLANCY.
Tuesday 9pm	RUNTS ON THE STOAD: The Cunning Stunts, an all-female co-operative theatrical company from England.
Wednesday 9pm	SEAN O'CASEY — Adaptations.
Thursday 9pm	FREDDY WHITE.
Friday 9pm	U2.
Saturday	THE RICHARD H. JONES BAND.

Belfast

Belfast city centre

Ulster Hall

U2 played here on 17 December 1980. This venue hosted other such artists as blues guitarist Rory Gallagher, The Rolling Stones (on 31 July 1964) and Led Zeppelin (on 5 March 1971).

LOCATION: 34 Bedford Street, Belfast, Co. Antrim

Bono, Larry and Adam at Ulster Hall, December 1980

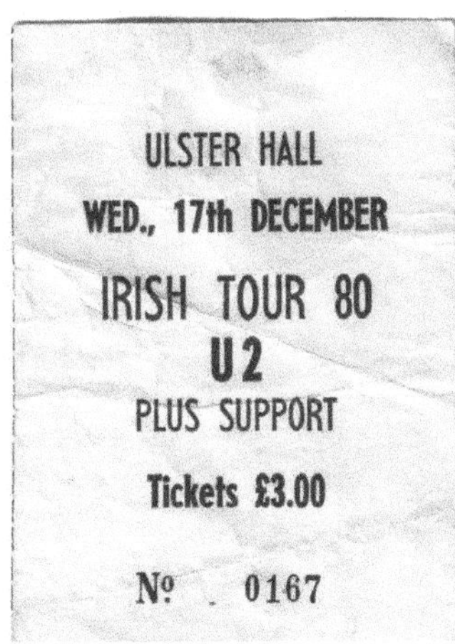
ULSTER HALL
WED., 17th DECEMBER
IRISH TOUR 80
U2
PLUS SUPPORT
Tickets £3.00
Nº . 0167

Belfast city centre
Queens University

U2 played here on the following dates:
15 November 1979 (U2 opened for Squeeze on this occasion, playing in the Speakeasy Hall);
1 February 1980 (they played at the Students' Union Ball in the Speakeasy Hall on this occasion, and, being fifth on the bill, they came after The Undertones and Stiff Little Fingers); 23 January 1981 (in the McMordie Hall; now called the Mandela Hall).
LOCATION: Belfast, ('Q.U.B.'), University Road, Belfast, BT7 1NN, Co. Antrim

Balmoral
Kings Hall

There is a small hall to the rear of the King's Hall called the Balmoral Hall, where, on 8 March 1987, U2 filmed six songs for the *Old Grey Whistle Test*, but only two songs were aired – 'Exit' and 'In God's Country'. This smaller venue is often referred to as the Balmoral TV Studios. U2 played here with Lou Reed on 24 June 1987. This venue, and the agricultural showgrounds and hall are similar to Dublin's Royal Dublin Society (RDS) and have hosted many bands, most notably The Beatles on 2 November 1964.
LOCATION: The Balmoral Hall, (part of King's Hall), Balmoral, Belfast BT9 6GW, Co. Antrim

Belfast city centre
Waterfront

On 18 May 1998, Bono and The Edge joined Ash on stage for one song during the Yes Campaign concert – a concert aimed at raising support for the referendum on the Belfast agreement. Larry and Adam then joined the rest of the band on stage for two songs – 'Stand By Me' and 'One'.
LOCATION: 2 Lanyon Place, Belfast, BT1 3WH, Co. Antrim

Bono at Queens University, January 1981

Londonderry

Coleraine

NUU Coleraine

One other place in the North of Ireland that U2 played was Londonderry – the topmost point – at NUU Coleraine (now known as UU Coleraine). They played there on 20 November 1979, opening for Squeeze.

Above: The Blue Lagoon. Below: publicity for U2's Irish tour of May 1980

Sligo

Strandhill

Baymount Hotel

U2 played here on 19 December 1980.

Doorly Park

The Blue Lagoon

U2 played here on two dates in 1980: 18 February and 12 May.

Mayo

Ballina

Town Hall Theatre

This was the venue for a U2 gig on 10 May 1980. The support act on this occasion was Myster Men. It was an eventful gig as a fight starts after the show, and one of U2's crew got his head smashed against a wall. The band came out to help and joined in the fight. Someone slammed a chair across Bono's

back; Adam's glasses were broken. The police eventually arrived, and the fight ended. Backstage, Bono lay on the ground, repeating 'I can't believe it!'. He told a local reporter that U2 would probably never play in Ballina again, and that other rock bands probably won't either.
LOCATION: Town Hall Theatre, Ballina, Co. Mayo

Donegal

Meenaleck Gwedore

Leo's Tavern

Leo's Tavern, both outside (above) and in (below)

From 11 to 13 December, 1985, U2 went to an area called Gweedore in Donegal where they rehearsed and practiced some new songs, and Bono recorded his duet with the band Clannad, 'In A Lifetime'. The pub, Leo's Tavern, owned by the Brennan Family, who are also members of the band Clannad, welcomed Bono behind the bar on one of these evenings to help pour a few pints.

Bono explains the video for 'In A Lifetime' in *U2 by U2*: 'I am the man who can't say no, and I loved Maire Ni Bhraonain [Clannad's singer]. I think she has one of the greatest voices the human ear has ever experienced. And I had a great time making the video. I was driving a Humber Super Snipe at the time, which was a big old bus of a thing, and I had bought a hearse version for spare parts so, before we carved it up, I thought I'd take it for a spin in the video.'
LOCATION: Leo's Tavern, Meenaleck Gwedore, Co. Donegal

Address and transport details

The Abbey Theatre 26/27 Lower Abbey Street Dublin 1 Telephone: 01 8787222 Fax: 018729177 Website:www. abbeytheatre.ie		Bus Routes: 1, 2, 3, 4, 4a, 5, 7a, 7, 7b, 7n, 7d, 8 LUAS: Abbey Street (Red Line), St Stephen's Green (Green Line) DART: Tara Street Parking: Irish Life Car Park
Adam's Childhood House 7 Ard na Mara Malahide Co. Dublin		Bus Route: 42 DART: Malahide
Adam's Current House Danesmoate House Rathfarnham Dublin 16		House located at foot of Dublin Mountains beside Taylors of Three Rock Pub Bus Routes: 14a, 14, 16, 16a, 48a, 75

The Ambassador O'Connell Street Dublin 1		The Edge joined Wyclef on stage here on 17th November 2002 Bus Routes: 1, 2, 3, 4, 4a, 5, 7, 7b, 7d, 7a, 7n, 8 LUAS: Abbey Street (Red Line), St Stephen's Green (Green Line) DART: Tara Street Car Parking: Arnott's Car Park
The Archway Temple Bar Dublin 2		Runs from Temple Bar to the Quays; U2 were famously photographed here. Bus Routes: 1, 2, 3, 4, 4a, 5, 7, 7d, 7n, 7b,7a, 8 LUAS: Jervis (Red Line), St Stephen's Green (Green Line) DART: Tara Street Parking: Fleet Street Car Park
All Saints ('Guinness') Church (Anglican Church) 403 Howth Road Raheny, Dublin 5 Telephone: 018313929 Website: www.allsaintsraheny.org		The church in Raheny where Bono was married Bus Routes: 29a, 29n, 31b, 31, 32, 32a, 32b, 42a, 42b DART: Raheny

U2 locations

Ardmore Studios Herbert Road Bray Co. Wicklow Telephone: 01 2862971 Fax: 01 2861894 Website: www.ardmore.ie	 	Bono joined The Corrs on stage here in 2002 This is also the venue where the video for 'With Or Without You' was filmed Bus Routes: 45a, 145, 185
Asgard Hotel Balscadden Road Howth Dublin 13	Now an apartment complex, this hotel was owned by Thin Lizzy's Phil Lynott, while Bono's father owned one of the apartments after it ceased to be a hotel Bus Route: 31	
The Baggot Inn (now Xico, a Mexican restaurant) 143 Lower Baggot Street, Dublin 2	 	Bus Routes: 1, 2, 3, 4a, 4, 5, 7a, 7b, 7, 7d, 8, 10 LUAS: St Stephen's Green (Green Line), Abbey Street (Red Line) DART: Pearse Street Car Parking: Dawson Car Park
Bagnalls Mullingar Dublin Road Rochfortbridge Co. Westmeath Telephone: 044 9224530	An early gig venue for U2 (long closed)	

Balgriffin Cemetary Balgriffin Dublin 17 Telephone: 01 8906287	Bono's parents are buried here Bus Routes: 42, 43 Train: Northern Suburban train	
Barretstown Castle Ballymore Eustace Co. Kildare Telephone: 045 864115 Fax: 045 864197 Website: www. bafrretstown.org e-mail: info@ barretstown.org		The Edge performed here with Paul McCartney as part of a charity concert
Bewleys Cafe 78/79 Grafton Street Dublin 2 Telephone: 01 6727720 e-mail: gs@ bewleys.ie Website: www. bewleys.com Opening hours: Monday– Wednesday 8am–10pm; Thursday-Saturday 8am–11pm; Sunday 9am–10pm		Famous Irish coffee shop, located in the centre of Dublin's Grafton Street Bus Routes: 1, 2, 3, 4, 4a, 5, 7, 7a, 7d, 7b, 7n, 8 LUAS: St Stephen's Green (Green Line) Jervis (Red Line) Parking: Brown Thomas Car Park or St Stephen's Green Shopping Centre

Blackrock Clinic Rock Road Blackrock Co. Dublin Telephone: 01 2832222 Fax: 01 2064314 Website: www.blackrock-clinic.ie		The hospital Bono attended for an operation on his sinuses on 7th February, 1999 Located on the Rock Road, Blackrock beside Blackrock College Bus Routes: 4, 4a, 5, 7, 7n, 7a, 8, 17, 44n, 45, 46e, 114 DART: Blackrock
Blackrock Park Rock Road Blackrock Co. Dublin Telephone: 01 2845066		U2 played an open-air gig here in 1978 Bus Routes: 4, 4A, 5, 7, 7A, 7N, 8, 17, 44N, 45, 46E, 114 DART: Blackrock
The Blue Lagoon Riverside Co. Sligo (now defunct)	U2 played here in 1980 on two occasions	
Blue Light Pub Barnacullia Sandyford Dublin 18 Telephone: 01 2954682		Adam Clayton was arrested here for drug possession; the pub is located at the foot of the Dublin Mountains Bus Route: 44B

Boland's Mill Grand Canal Dock Dublin 2	 	Adam celebrated his birthday here in 1987. It is located on the corner of Pearse Street and Barrow Street, very near The Factory Studios Bus Routes: 1, 2, 3, 4a, 4, 5, 7, 7a, 8, 13, 13a, 27x LUAS: Spencer Dock (Red Line) DART: Grand Canal Dock, St Stephen's Green (Green Line) Parking: Grand Canal Square car park
Bonavox 9 North Earl Street Dublin 1 Telephone: 01 874 2341 Email: info@bonavox.ie Website: www.bonavox.ie	 	Located on North Earl Street, this is where Bono got his stage name Bus Routes: 1, 2, 3, 4a, 4, 5, 7b, 7d, 7a, 7n, 8 LUAS: Abbey Street (Red Line), St Stephen's Green (Green Line) Parking: Irish Life Car Park
Bono's Childhood House (1) 36 Dale Road Stillorgan Co. Dublin	Bono lived here for the first eight weeks of his life Bus Routes: 5, 11, 44n, 46b, 47, 75, 116 LUAS: Kilmacud (Green Line)	

U2 locations

Bono's Childhood House (2) 10 Cedarwood Road Ballymun Dublin 9		Where Bono spent most of his childhood years Bus Routes: 13A, 13, 17A, 19, 19A, 104, 220
Bono's Current House Vico Road Killiney Co. Dublin		The DART to Killiney will take you near to Vico Road. Coming out from the train station, turn right. After about ten minutes' walk, you''ll come to a crossroads; from there you'll see Bono's house Parking: Killiney Station Car Park
Botanic Gardens College Park Botanic Avenue Belfast BT7 1LP Co. Antrim Telephone: 0044 28 9031 4762 or 0044 7767 271683 (Monday to Friday, 9am–4.30pm only)		U2 performed here in August 1997

The Burlington Hotel Upper Leeson Street Dublin 4 Telephone: 01 6185600 Fax: 01 6184583 e-mail: info@burlingtonhotel.ie Website: www.burlingtonhotel.ie		U2 performed here as part of the launch of Gangs of New York film Bus Routes: 7d, 7b, 10, 11b, 11a, 11, 14a, 14, 15a, 15b, 15, 18 LUAS: Charlemont (Green Line) Parking: Ranelagh Public Car Park
Cafe Club H Hanover Quay Dublin 2		U2 had their Christmas party here in December 2011 Bus Routes: 1, 2, 3, 4, 4a, 5, 7, 7a, 8, 27x, 45, 50 DART: Grand Canal Dock LUAS: Spenser Dock (Red Line)
Captain Americas 44 Grafton Street Dublin 2 Telephone: 01 6715266 email: dublin@captainamericas.com Website: www.captainamericas.com/grafton		Bus Routes: 1, 2, 3, 4a, 4, 5, 7b, 7d, 7n, 7a, 7, 8 LUAS: St Stephen's Green (Green Line), Jervis (Red Line) Parking: Brown Thomas Car Park St Stephen's Green Shopping Centre Car Park

U2 locations

Castle Park School Castle Park Road Dalkey Co. Dublin Telephone: 01 2803037 Website: www. castleparkschool.ie e-mail: admin@ castleparkschool.ie		Adam's first School Bus Routes: 7d, 8, 59 DART: Glenageary
Christ Church Cathedral Christchurch Place Dublin 8 Telephone: 01 6778099 Fax: 01 6798991 e-mail: angela. mcgroggan@ cccdub.ie Website: welcome@ cccdub.ie		Bus Routes: 7d, 7b, 10, 11b, 11a, 11, 14, 14a, 15f, 15n, 15b, 15a LUAS: Four Courts (Red Line), St Stephen's Green (Green Line) Parking: Christchurch Car Park

Church of the Assumption St Mary's Road Howth Co. Dublin Telephone: 018397398 Fax: 01 8397398 e-mail: assumptionhowth@eircom.net Website: www.howthparish.ie	U2 attended the funeral of Bill Graham here in 1996 DART: Howth Station
Church of the Holy Ghost, Dennehy's Cross, Cork May be referred to as The Church of the Holy Spirit Telephone: 021 434 4452 e-mail: holyspiritparish@eircom.net Website: www.dennehyscrossparish.ie	The funeral mass of Rory Gallagher took place here

City Hall
(Cork City Council)
Anglesea Street
Cork
Telephone:
021 4966222
Fax: 021 4314238
Website: www.
corkcity.ie

A venue for U2 in 1982

Claddagh Hall
Co. Galway

U2 performed at a benefit gig here in 1979

The Clarence Hotel
6-8 Wellington Quay
Dublin 2
Telephone:
01 4070800
Fax: 01 4070820
e-mail:
reservations@
theclarence.ie
Website: www.
theclarence.ie

Bono & Edge's hotel
Bus Routes: 1, 2, 3, 4a, 4, 5, 7d, 7, 7a, 7n, 7b, 8
LUAS: Jervis (Red Line), St Stephen's Green (Green Line)
Parking: Jervis Street Car Park

Coach House Pub
Ballinteer Avenue
Ballinteer
Dublin 16
Telephone: 01
2987088
Website: www.
thecoach.ie

Where Guggi and occasionally Bono drinks
Bus Routes: 14A, 14, 16A, 16, 48A, 75, 116
LUAS Stop: Balally (Green Line)

U2 locations

Community Centre Balscadden Road Howth Dublin 13	U2 gigged here on 11 July 1979 Bus Route: 31	
County Club Montenotte Cork City Co. Cork (now The Montenotte Hotel) General Information: info@themontenottehotel.com Website: www.themontenottehotel.com	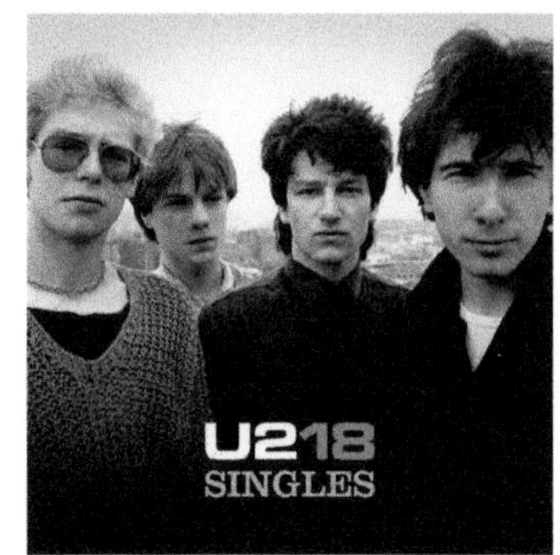	U2 played here in 1980. Cover photo of *U218* was taken on the roof of this venue
Cowper Street Dublin 7	Where Bono's mother was from Bus Routes:10, 25, 25a, 26, 37, 37x, 39b, 39x, 39a, 39c, 39, 66b LUAS:Museum (Red Line)	
Crofton Airport Hotel, Upper Drumcondra Road Drumcondra Dublin 9 – now The Dublin Skylon Hotel Telephone: 01 8843900 e-mail: reservations@dublinskylonhotel.com Website: www.dublinskylonhotel.com		U2 played at the Crofton Airport Hotel in September 1978 Bus Routes: 3, 11, 11b, 11a, 13a, 16a, 16, 33, 41, 41b, 41c, 746

Croke Park Stadium 3 Jones' Road Dublin 3 Telephone: 01 8192300 e-mail: info@ crokepark.ie Website: www. crokepark.ie		U2 gig venue for The Joshua Tree Tour, Vertigo Tour and 360° Tour Bus Routes: 3, 11b, 11a, 11, 13, 13a, 16a, 16, 20b, 27b, 29a LUAS: Connolly (Red Line)
The Custom House Custom House Quay, Dublin 1, Telephone: 01 8882000/8882538		A government building that was gutted in the Civil War of 1922 Bus Routes: 1, 2, 3, 4a, 4, 5, 7n, 7d, 7a, 7b, 7, 8 LUAS: Busáras (Red Line), St Stephen's Green (Green Line) DART: Tara Street Parking: City Quay Car Park
Dalymount Stadium Dalymount Park Prospect Road Phibsborough Dublin 7 Telephone: 011 8680923 Fax: 01 8686460 e-mail: info@ bohemians.ie Websites: www. stadiumguide.com www.bohemians.ie		U2 played a gig here on 29 July 1980 Bus Routes: 4, 4a, 10, 13, 19, 19a, 38c, 38b, 38a, 38, 39x, 40

U2 locations

Dave Fanning's Childhood House 54 Foster Avenue Mount Merrion Co. Dublin	Dave Fanning was the DJ who discovered U2. Bus Routes: 17, 46B DART: Booterstown Car Parking: Radisson St Helen's Car Park	
Derrick Nealson Marley Park Rathfarnham Dublin 16 Telephone: 01 4942741	U2's go-to guitar repair guy Bus Routes: 14, 14a, 16, 16a, 48a, 75, 116, 161 Parking: Marley Park Car Park	
The Arcadia (also known as UCC Downtown Kampus), Lower Glanmie Road, Cork now The Arcadia Hall Apartments	U2 gigged here on 20th December 1980	
Dublin Castle ('Dubh Linn') Castle Street Dublin 2 Telephone: 01 6458813		Where Dublin was founded Bus Routes: 1, 2, 3, 4, 4A, 5, 7A, 7D, 7N, 7B, 7, LUAS: Jervis (Red Line), St Stephen's Green (Green Line) DART: Tara Street Car Parking: Christchurch Car Park
Dublin Institute of Technology Bolton Street Dublin 1 Website: www.dit.ie		U2 played a lunctime rag-week gig here in 1979 Bus Routes: 1, 2, 3, 4a, 4, 5, 7, 7d, 7b, 7a, 8, 10 LUAS: Jervis (Red Line), St Stephen's Green (Green Line) Parking: Parnell Centre Car Park

Eamonn Doran's Crown Alley Temple Bar Dublin 2 now The Old Storehouse Bar and Restaurant Telephone: 01 6074003 e-mail: info@theoldstorehouse.ie Website: www.theoldstorehouse.ie		Bono and The Edge performed here in 2000 Bus Routes: 1, 2, 3, 4, 4a, 5, 7, 7d, 7n, 7b,7a, 8 LUAS: Jervis (Red Line), St Stephen's Green (Green Line) DART: Tara Street Parking: Fleet Street Car Park
Eastlink Bridge North Wall Quay Dublin 1		As featured in the 'Pride (In The Name of Love)' video Bus Route: 1, 2, 3, 50, 53, 53a, 56a, 74a, 74, 77, 77a, 90 LUAS: The Point (Red Line) DART: Grand Canal Dock Parking: Point Village Car Park
Easons Bookshop 40 Lower O'Connell Street, Dublin 1 Telephone: 01 8583800 Fax: 01 8583806 Website: www.easons.ie e-mail: customer service@easons.com		U2 did a book signing here for U2 by U2 Bus Routes: 1, 2, 3, 4, 4a, 5, 7, 7b, 7d, 7a, 7n, 8 LUAS: Abbey Street (Red Line), St Stephen's Green (Green Line) DART: Tara Street Parking: Arnott's Car Park

U2 locations

The Edge's Childhood House 10 St Margaret's Park, Malahide Co. Dublin		Bus Route: 42 DART: Malahide
The Edge's former residence: Sorrento Cottage, Sorrento Terrace, Dalkey Co. Dublin		DART: Dalkey Car Parking: Dalkey Station Car Park
The Edge's former residence: Martello Tower Malahide Co. Dublin		

'Elsinore' 7a Coliemore Road Dalkey Co. Dublin	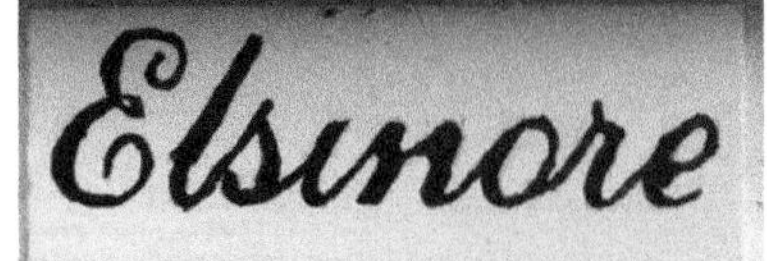 	Where some of the writing for *Achtung Baby* took place in early 1991 DART: Dalkey Car Parking: Dalkey Station Car Park
The Factory 35 A Barrow Street Ringsend Dublin 4	 	One of U2's old Rehearsal Studios DART: Grand Canal and 200 metres to the left. Bus Routes: Pearse Street/Grand Canal Dock: 1, 2, 3, 50, 56\a, 74, 74a, 77, 77a Grand Canal Street (Mount Street Stop): 4/a, 7, 7a
Fitzwilliam Square Dublin 2		Video for 'Sweetest Thing' filmed here Bus Routes: 4a, 4, 5, 7, 7a, 7b, 7d, 8, 10, 11b, 11a, 11 LUAS: Charlemont (Green Line), Abbey Street (Red Line) DART: Pearse Street Parking: On-street parking; Conrad Hotel Car Park

U2 locations

The Gaiety Theatre
South King Street
Dublin 2
Telephone: 01 677 1921 / 6771717/ 6795622
Website: www.gaietytheatre.ie

Bono's father sang here. Video for the end of 'Sometimes...' shot here
Bus Routes: 1, 2, 3, 4a, 4, 5, 7, 7n, 7d, 7b, 7a, 8
LUAS: St Stephen's Green (Green Line) Jervis (Red Line)
DART: Pearse Street
Parking:
Fitzwilliam Hotel Car Park
St Stephen's Green Shopping Centre car Park

Garden of Eden
Tullamore
Co. Offaly

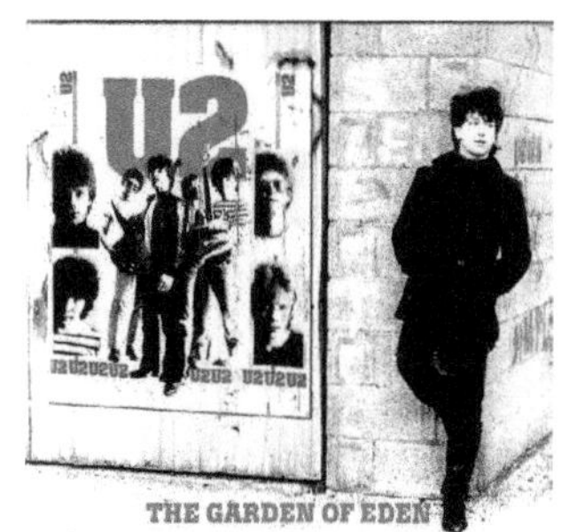

U2 gigged here on 11th May 1980

Glasnevin National School
Botanic Avenue
Glasnevin
Dublin 9
Telephone: 01 8373727

Bono's primary school
Sometimes referred to as The Inkpot
Bus Routes: 4, 4a, 11, 11b, 11a, 13, 13a, 19a, 19, 40d, 40a, 40

Address and transport details

Hanover Quay Dublin 4		Hanover Quay is where U2's current studios (HQ) are housed. The quay itself is also where the *October* album was shot and where the video for 'Gloria' was filmed Bus Routes: 1, 2, 3, 4, 4a, 5, 7, 7a, 8, 27x, 45, 50 DART: Grand Canal Dock LUAS: Spenser Dock (Red Line)
Ha'penny Bridge Dublin 2		U2 were photographed here Bus Routes: 1, 2, 3, 4, 4a, 5, 7, 7d, 7n, 7b,7a, 8 LUAS: Jervis (Red Line), St Stephen's Green (Green Line) DART: Tara Street Parking: Fleet Street Car Park
Harcourt Hotel 60 Harcourt Street Dublin 2 Telephone: 01 4783677 Fax: 01 4781557 email: reservations@ harcourthotel.ie website: www. harcourthotel.ie		Formally 'Keystone Studios' Bus Routes: 7d, 7b, 10, 11, 11b, 11a, 14, 14a, 15b, 15, 15e LUAS: Harcourt (Green Line), Jervis (Red Line) Parking: Hilton Hotel Car Park

U2 locations

Hard Rock Cafe 12 Fleet Street Temple Bar Dublin 2 Telephone: 01 6717777 Fax: 01 6717711 e-mail: info@hardrockcafe.ie	 	Trabant from Zoo TV tour can be found here Bus Routes: 1, 2, 3, 4, 4a, 5, 7, 7d, 7n, 7b,7a, 8 LUAS: Jervis (Red Line), St Stephen's Green (Green Line) DART: Tara Street Parking: Fleet Street Car Park
HMV 65 Grafton Street Dublin 2 Telephone: 01 6795334	 	Bus Routes: 1, 2, 3, 4a, 4, 5, 7b, 7d, 7n, 7a, 7, 8 LUAS: St Stephen's Green (Green Line), Jervis (Red Line) Parking: Brown Thomas Car Park St Stephen's Green Shopping Centre Car Park
HQ Club 57 Middle Abbey Street, Dublin 1 now The Academy Telephone: 01 877 9999 e-mail: info@theacademydublin.com Website: www.theacademydublin.com	Bono performed here in 1999 Bus Routes: 1, 2, 3, 4, 4a, 5, 7a, 7d, 7b, 7n, 7, 8 LUAS: Jervis (Red Line), St Stephen's Green (Green Line) DART: Tara Street Parking: Arnotts Car Park	

Irish Times Offices 24-28 Tara Street Dublin 2 Telephone: 01 6758000 Website: www.irishtimes.com	Bus Routes: 1, 2, 3, 4, 4a, 5, 7, 7d, 7b, 7n, 7a, 8 LUAS: Abbey Street (Red Line), St Stephen's Green (Green Line) DART: Tara Street Parking: Apollo Car Park	
Jackie Lennox's Chipper 137 Bandon Road Cork Telephone. 021 431 6118		The ownser bought a U2 War Gold Disc for charity and Bono presented the disc to him.
Johnnie Fox's Pub Glencullen Road Glencullen Co. Dublin Telephone: 01 2955647 Fax: 01 2958911 e-mail: info@jfp.ie Website: www.jfp.ie		Adam appeared on an Irish TV programme, filmed here in 1990 discussing Irish Tradtional Music Bus Route: 44B
Kilmainham Jail Inchicore Road Kilmainham Dublin 8 Telephone: 01 4535984 Fax: 01 4532037 Email: kilmainhamgaol@opw.ie Web: www.heritageireland.ie		Bus Routes: 19, 25, 25a, 26, 51c, 51b, 51d, 66, 66d, 66b, 66a, 67, 79, 79a LUAS: Suir Road (Red Line)

U2 locations

The Balmoral Hall (part of King's Hall) Balmoral, Belfast BT9 6GW Co. Antrim Referred to as Balmoral TV Studios Telephone: 0044 28 9066 5225 Fax: 0044 28 9066 1264 e-mail:. info@ kingshall.co.uk Website: www. kingshall.co.uk		U2 played here for *The Old Grey Whistle Test* in 1987 and also with Lou Reed on 24th June 1987
Lansdowne Road (Aviva Stadium) Dublin 4 Telephone: 01 2382300 Fax: 01 2382333 e-mail: info@ avivastadium.ie Website: www. avivastadium.ie		Venue of Popmart Tour Bus Routes: 1, 2, 3, 4a, 4, 5, 7a, 7, 7n, 8, 18, 27x DART: Lansdowne Road
Larry Mullen's Childhood House 60 Rosemount Avenue Artane Dublin 5		Bus Routes: 27x, 27, 27b, 29a, 31b, 31, 32b, 32, 32a, 42, 42a, 42b DART: Harmonstown

Larry Mullen's Current House Claremont Lodge Claremont Road Howth Co. Dublin		Where Larry lives in Howth. Note it's a private road, and has limited access Bus Routes: 31, 31B DART: Sutton
Leisureland Salthill Co. Galway Telephone: 091 521455 Fax: 091 521093 e-mail: leisureland@galwaycity.ie Website: www.leisureland.ie		U2 gigged here on 18 December 1980
Leo's Tavern Meenaleck Gwedore Co. Donegal Telephone: 074 95 48143 Email: info@leostavern.com		From 11–13 December 1985, U2 went here to write and rehearse, with Bono helping out with pints on one occasion in Leo's bar

U2 locations

<table>
<tr><td>Leixlip Castle
Main Street
Leixlip
Co. Kildare
Telephone: 01 6244430
Fax: 01 6244446</td><td></td><td>U2 gigged here on 27 July 1980</td></tr>
<tr><td>Liberty Hall
Eden Quay
Dublin 1
Website: www.libertyhall.ie</td><td colspan="2">U2 play a benefit gig here in 1978
Bus Routes:
1, 2, 3, 4, 4a, 5, 7a., 7d, 7, 7a, 7b, 8
LUAS: Abbey Street (Red Line), St Stephen's Green (Green Line)
DART: Tara Street
Parking:
Irish Life Car Park</td></tr>
<tr><td>Lillie's Bordello
Adam Court
6 Grafton Street
Dublin 2
Telephone: 01 6799204/01 679 9204
e-mail: guestlist@lilliesbordello.ie
Website: www.lilliesbordello.ie</td><td></td><td>Bus Routes: 1, 2, 3, 4, 4a, 5, 7a., 7d, 7, 7a, 7b, 8
LUAS: St Stephen's Green (Green Line), Abbey Street (Red Line)
DART: Tara Street
Parking: Brown Thomas Car Park. St Stephen's Green Car Park</td></tr>
<tr><td>Lock's Restaurant
1 Windsor Terrace
Portobello
Dublin 8
Telephone: 01 4200555
Fax : 01 4200557
Website: www.locksbrasserie.com</td><td>
</td><td>Where U2 and their staff at Principle Management had a Christmas lunch in 2007
Bus Routes: 14, 14a, 15b, 15a, 15f, 15, 16, 16a, 19, 19a, 44
LUAS: Harcourt (Green Line)</td></tr>
</table>

Magnet Bar
130 Pearse Street
Dublin 2
(Long closed)

U2 played here on several occasions
Opposite a hotel called the Pearse Hotel
Bus Routes: 1, 2, 3, 4a, 4, 5, 7b, 7, 7a, 7d, 8, 10
LUAS: Mayor Square – NCI (Red Line), St Stephen's Green (Green Line)
DART:
Pearse Street
Parking:
Grand Canal Square Car Park

Manhattan Lounge
Co. Galway

U2 played here on 18 March 1979

Marine Hotel
Sutton Cross
Sutton
Dublin 13
Telephone: 01 8390000
Fax: 01 8390442
e-mail: info@marinehotel.ie
Website: www.marinehotel.ie

U2 played here in 1977
Bus Routes: 31, 31b, 102
DART: Sutton

Maysfield Leisure Centre
49 East Bridge Street, Belfast, BT1 3NR, Co. Antrim
Telephone: 0044 28 9024 1633

U2 played here in 1982

U2 locations

McDonald's 10-11 Grafton Street Dublin 2 Telephone: 01 6778393 Fax: 01 6795550 Website: www.mcdonalds.ie	Bono, in his youth, caused a stir reading the Bible there Bus Routes: 1, 2, 3, 4a, 4, 5, 7b, 7d, 7n, 7a, 7, 8 LUAS: St Stephen's Green (Green Line), Jervis (Red Line) Parking: Brown Thomas Car Park St Stephen's Green Shopping Centre Car Park	
McGonagle's 27 South Anne Street Dublin 2 (Long-closed)	An early gig venue for U2, where U2's DJ friend, Dave Fanning also used to play Bus Routes: 1, 2, 3, 4a, 4, 5, 7b, 7d, 7n, 7a, 7, 8 LUAS: St Stephen's Green (Green Line) Jervis (Red Line) Parking: Brown Thomas Car Park St Stephen's Green Shopping Centre Car Park	
Mojos 4 Merchant's Arch Temple Bar Dublin 2 Telephone: 01 6727905		Some great U2 related material can be bought here Bus Routes: 1, 2, 3, 4, 4a, 5, 7, 7d, 7n, 7b,7a, 8 LUAS: Jervis (Red Line), St Stephen's Green (Green Line) DART: Tara Street Parking: Fleet Street Car Park
Mother Redcaps Christchurch Back Lane Dublin 8		A very old pub, closed since 2005 Bus Routes: 7d, 7b, 10, 11b, 11a, 11, 14, 14a, 15f, 15n, 15b, 15a LUAS: Four Courts (Red Line), St Stephen's Green (Green Line) Parking: Christchurch Car Park

Mount Temple Comprehensive School 128 Malahide Road Clontarf Dublin 3 Telephone: 01 8336984 e-mail: info@mounttemple.ie Website: www.mounttemple.ie		Where U2 met as schoolboys Bus Routes: 20b, 27x, 27, 27b, 29n, 29a, 31b, 31, 32a, 32b, 32, 32x DART: Clontarf Road
Moydrum Castle Moydrum		This castle appears on the cover of the album *The Unforgettable fire*
National Stadium/ Boxing Arena 8 South Circular Road, Dublin 8 Telephone: 01 4533371 Fax: 01 4540777 e-mail: info@iaba.ie Website: www.nationalstadium.ie		Early gig venue for U2 Bus Routes: 16a, 16, 17, 19, 19a, 49a, 49, 50, 54n, 54a, 56a, 77a LUAS: Fatima (Red Line), Harcourt (Green Line)
Nude/Mr. Pussy's/ Toscas Restaurants 21 Suffolk Street Dublin 2 (all closed)	Bus Routes: 1, 2, 3, 4a, 4, 5, 7b, 7d, 7n, 7, 7a, 8 LUAS: St Stephen's Green (Green Line) Abbey Street (Red Line) DART: Tara Street Parking: Brown Thomas Car Park	

U2 locations

NUU, Coleraine
University of Ulster
Coleraine Campus
Cromore Road
BT52 1SA
Co. Londonderry
(Now UU Coleraine)
Telephone: 0044 28 70123456
Website: www.ulster.ac.uk/campus/coleraine

U2 played here in 1979

O'Donoghue's Pub
15 Merrion Row
Dublin 2
Telephone: 01 6607194
Fax: 01 6614303
e-mail: odonogues dublin@eircom.net
Website: www.odonoghues.ie

Bono had a pint with actor Sean Penn, in this pub
Bus Routes: 1, 2, 3, 4a, 4, 5, 7n, 7, 7b, 7a, 7d
LUAS: St Stephen's Green (Green Line), Abbey Street (Red Line)
DART: Pearse Street
Parking: Dawson Car Park

Olympia Theatre
72 Dame Street
Dublin 2
Telephone: 01 6793323
Fax: 01 6799576
Website: www.olympia.ie

In 1993, Larry, The Edge & Bono joined Johnny Cash on stage here
Bus Routes: 1, 2, 3, 4a, 4, 5, 7s, 7n, 7, 7a, 7b, 8
LUAS: Jervis (Red Line), St Stephen's Green (Green Line)
DART: Tara Street
Parking: Trinity Street Car Park

Cork Opera House Emmet Place Cork City Telephone: 021 4270022/ 021 4274308 Website: www.corkoperahouse.ie		U2 gigged here on 5th December 1979
The Oscar Theatre Sandymount Avenue Dublin 4 (Now the Y.M.C.A. Sports Grounds)		U2 held rehearsals for *The Unforgettable Fire* here from 6–13 October 1984 Bus Routes: 2, 3, 4a, 4, 5, 7a, 7, 8, 18, 27x, 45 DART: Sandymount
Pairc Uí Chaoimh Ballintemple Cork City, Co. Cork Telephone: 021 4963311 Email: administrator.cork@gaa.ie Website: www.gaacork.ie		U2 played here on 8 August 1987 and again on 24 August 1993
Patrick Guilbaud's Restaurant 21 Merrion Street Upper, Dublin 2 Telephone: 01 6764192 Website: www.restaurantpatrickguilbaud.ie	One of Bono's favourite restaurants, located by the Merrion Hotel. Bus Routes: 1, 2, 3, 4, 4a, 5, 7, 7d, 7a, 7b, 8, 10 LUAS: St Stephen's Green (Green Line), Abbey Street (Red Line) DART: Pearse Street Parking: Dawson Car Park	

U2 locations

Phoenix Park Race-Course Navan Road Castleknock Dublin 15 (No longer a race-course, it is now apartment buildings)	U2 played here on 14 August 1983 The site can be found by taking the N3 (Navan Road) and is on the city side of the M50/Blanchardstown roundabout Bus Routes: 37, 38, 38a, 38b, 38c, 39, 39a, 39c, 39b, 70, 70a, 70b Parking: Rathborne Village Car Park
Pink Elephant Nightclub 35-37 South Frederick Street Dublin 2	 Bono appeared here on stage in 1989 as part of Gavin Friday's album release
The POD 35 Harcourt Street Dublin 2 (Currently closed)	Where the 'Hold Me Thrill Me Kiss Me Kill Me' single was launched. Bono joined Prince on stage here on one occasion Bus Routes: 7d, 7b, 10, 11, 11b, 11a, 14, 14a, 15b, 15, 15e LUAS: Harcourt (Green Line), Jervis (Red Line) Parking: Hilton Hotel Car Park
The Point Depot/ The O2, North Wall Quay, Dublin 1 Telephone: 01 8198888 Website: www.theo2.ie	U2 played a series of gigs here in 1989. It is now known as the O2. Bus Routes: 1, 2, 3, 50, 53, 53a, 56a, 74a, 74, 77, 77a, 90 LUAS: The Point (Red Line) DART: Grand Canal Dock Parking: Point Village Car Park
Presbyterian Church Hall Howth, Co. Dublin Telephone: 01 8323198 Website: www.hmpchurch.org	Where U2 played their first ever gig under the name U2 Bus Route: 31

Principle Management 30/32 Sir John Rogerson's Quay Dublin 2 (opposite the Samuel Beckett Bridge) Telephone: 01 6777330 Fax: 01 6777276	U2's management Bus Routes: 1, 2, 3, 4, 4a, 7, 7a, 8, 13, 13a, 27x, 44b LUAS: Spencer Dock (Red Line), St Stephen's Green (Green Line) DART: Pearse Street Parking: Grand Canal Square Car Park	
Punchestown Racecourse Punchestown Naas, Co. Kildare Telephone: 045 897704 Fax: 045 897319 Website: www.punchestown-festival.com	U2 played here on 18th July 1982 30 miles from Dublin Airport (M50, N7, R410) 22 miles from Dublin City (N7, R410). Take N7 (Naas Road) to traffic lights at Naas. Turn left at lights (R410) At approx. two miles turn right at the junction. After approx. one mile, you'll find the racecourse gates on the left	
The Purty Loft/ Kitchen 3-4 Old Dunleary Road, Dún Laoghaire, Co. Dublin Telephone: 01 2843576 Website: www.purtykitchen.com		Early gig venue of U2 Bus Routes: 7, 7a, 7n, 8, 46a, 46n, 75, 746 DART: Salthill & Monkstown Parking: West Pier Car Park
The Queen's of Dalkey 12 Castle Street Dalkey, Co. Dublin Telephone: 01 2854569 email: info@thequeens.ie Website: www.thequeens.ie		Bono's local bar Bus Routes: 7d, 8, 59 DART: Dalkey Parking: Eurostar Car Park

U2 locations

Queens University Belfast University Road Belfast BT7 1NN Co. Antrim Telephone: 0044 2890 245133 Website: www.qub.ac.uk		U2 played here on many occasions between 1979 and 1981
Registry Office (Civil Registrations Office) Sir Patrick Duns Hospital, Lower Grand Canal Street Dublin 2 Telephone: 01 6787114 Fax: 01 6787116		Where The Edge married Morleigh Steinberg Bus Routes: 1, 2, 3, 4, 4a, 5, 7b, 7, 8, 10, 13a, 13 LUAS: Spencer Dock (Red Linei), St Stephen's Green (Green Line) DART: Grand Canal Dock Parking: Grand Canal Square Car Park
Rory Gallagher Corner Temple Bar Dublin 2		Edge's tribute to blues guitarist, Rory Gallagher Bus Routes: 1, 2, 3, 4, 4a, 5, 7b, 7d, 7, 7a, 8 LUAS: Jervis (Red Line), St Stephen's Green (Green Line) DART: Tara Street Parking: Fleet Street Car Park

Rory Gallagher's Grave St Oliver's Cemetary Clash Road Model Farm Road Co. Cork		Grave of blues guitarist, Rory Gallagher. Adam and The Edge attended the funeral
Rotunda Hospital Parnell Street Dublin 1 Telephone: 01 8171700 Fax: 01 8726523 Website: www.rotunda.ie		Where Bono was born Bus Routes: 1, 2, 3, 4a, 4, 5, 7d, 7a, 7b, 7, 8, 10 LUAS: Abbey Street (Red Line), St Stephen's Green (Green Line) DART: Tara Street Parking: Findlater House Car Park
Royal Dublin Society (RDS) Ballsbridge Dublin 4 Telephone: 01 6680866 Fax: 01 6604014 email: info@rds.ie Website: www.rds.ie		Where the Zoo TV tour was hosted in Dublin Bus Routes: 2, 3, 4, 4a, 5, 7a, 7d, 7b, 8, 10, 18 DART: Sandymount
RTÉ Donnybrook Dublin 4 Website: www.RTÉ.ie	U2's first TV appearance was from here Bus Routes: 2, 3, 4a, 5, 7b, 7d, 7a, 7, 8, 10, 25x DART: Sydney Parade Parking: St Vincent's University Hospital	

U2 locations

Savoy Cinema 16-17 Upper O'Connell Street Dublin 1 Website: www.savoy.ie	 	Where *Rattle and Hum* was premiered Bus Routes: 1, 2, 3, 4, 4a, 5, 7, 7b, 7d, 7a, 7n, 8 LUAS: Abbey Street (Red Line), St Stephen's Green (Green Line) DART: Tara Street Parking: Arnott's Car Park
Savoy Hotel Henry Street Limerick City Co. Limerick Telephone: 061 448700 Website: www.savoylimerick.com	U2 gigged here on 18 March 1978	
SFX 23 Upper Sherrard Street Dublin 1 (Long closed; now apartments)	Early U2 gig venue Bus Routes: 1, 2, 3, 4a, 4, 5, 7d, 7a, 7b, 8, 10 LUAS: Connolly (Red Line) DART: Connolly Parking: Findlater House Car Park	
The Shelbourne Hotel 27 St Stephen's Green Dublin 2 Telephone: 01 6634500 Fax: 01 6616006 Website: www.shelbournehoteldublin.com		U2 attended a charity dinner here in 2004 Bus Routes: 1, 2, 3, 4, 4a, 5, 7, 7d, 7a, 7n, 7b, 8 LUAS: St Stephen's Green (Green Line), Abbey Street (Red Line) DART: Pearse Street Parking: Dawson Car Park

Sheriff Street Community Centre Sheriff Street Dublin 1		U2 played a free gig here in 1982
Slack Alice's Nightclub 57 O'Connell Street Upper Dublin 1 (Long closed)	U2 played here in April 1977	
Smithfield Plaza Dublin 7		U2 were awarded the Freedom of the City here in 2000
Solomon's 15 St Stephen's Green Dublin 2 (now The Little Museum of Dublin) email: info@ solomonfineart.ie Website: www. solomonfineart.ie		Currently a museum with great U2 exhibits and memorabilia Bus Routes: 1, 2, 3, 4a, 4, 5, 7d, 7a, 7n, 7, 7b, 8 LUAS: St Stephen's Green (Green Line) Abbey Street (Red Line) DART: Pearse Street Parking: Dawson Car Park

U2 locations

Slane Castle Slane Co. Meath Telephone: 041 9820643 Website: www.slanecastle.ie email: info@slanecastle.ie		Open for guided tours June–September (inclusive) 12–5pm; closed Friday and Saturdays
The Stardust 66 Grand Parade Greenmount Cork City Telephone: 021 4272068		U2 played here in their early days
The Stella Ballroom 16 Shannon Street Limerick City Co. Limerick (Now a Bingo hall)		U2 won the Harp Larger Contest here in 1978, winning the band studio time and £500
STS Studios 2 Cecilia Street Dublin 2		Bus Routes: 1, 2, 3, 4, 4a, 5, 7b, 7d, 7, 7a, 8 LUAS: Jervis (Red Line), St Stephen's Green (Green Line) DART: Tara Street Parking: Fleet Street Car Park

St Andrew's National School Church Road Malahide Co. Dublin Telephone: 01 8450185 Fax: 01 8230185 email: standrewsschool malahide@eircom.net Website: www. standrewsschool malahide.com		Edge's first school Bus Routes: 32a, 32x, 42, 102, 142 DART: Malahide
St Columba's College Kilmashogue Lane Whitechurch Rathfarnham Dublin 16 Telephone: 01 4906791 Fax: 01 4936655 email: admin@ stcolumbas.ie Website: www. stcolumbas.ie		The school Adam attended before going to Mount Temple Comprehensive School
St Fintan's School Sutton Dublin 13 Telephone: 01 8324632 Fax: 01 8393629 Website: www. stfintanshs.ie		Where U2 played their first gig (as Feedback) on 11 April 1977 Bus Routes: 31, 31b, 32, 32b, 32a, 102 DART: Sutton

U2 locations

St Mary's Church Knocksink Enniskerry Co. Wicklow Telephone: 01 2760030		Where The Edge married his first wife, Aislinn
St Stephen's Green Dublin 2 www. stephensgreen.com		Bus Routes: 1, 2, 3, 4, 4a, 5, 7a, 7, 7d, 7n, 7b, 8 LUAS: St Stephen's Green (Green Line) Jervis (Red Line) DART: Pearse Street Parking: Fitzwilliam Hotel Car Park
Suttonians RFC Station Road Sutton Dublin 13 Telephone: 01 8394790		U2 played here in 1977 Bus Routes: 31b, 31, 32b, 32, 102 DART: Sutton
Dandelion Market St Stephen's Green Dublin 2 Telephone: 01 4781233 Long closed; currently a TGI Fridays Website: www. fridays.ie		Bus Routes: 1, 2, 3, 4, 4a, 5, 7a, 7, 7d, 7n, 7b, 8 LUAS: St Stephen's Green (Green Line), Jervis (Red Line) DART: Pearse Street Parking: Fitzwilliam Hotel Car Park

Tivoli Theatre
135–138 Francis Street, Dublin 8
Telephone: 01 4544472
email: info@tivoli.ie
Website: www.tivoli.ie

Bus Routes: 51 B, 78A, 206, 121, 123, 51a
LUAS: Smithfield or Four Courts (Red Line), St Stephen's Green (Green Line)

The Top Hat Ballroom
Longford Place
Dún Laoghaire
Co. Dublin
(Long closed; now apartments)

Bus Routes: 7, 7a, 7n, 8, 46a, 46n, 75, 746
DART: Salthill & Monkstown
Parking: West Pier Car Park

Town Hall Theatre
Ballina
Co. Mayo

Gig venue for U2 on 10th May 1980

Trinity College
College Green
Dublin 2
Telephone:01 8961000
Website: www.tcd.ie

U2 played here on several occasions

TV Club
Harcourt Street
Dublin 2
Now a Police/Garda Station

U2 played at the TV Club (also known as Eamon Andrew's Studios) on 22 December 1980.
Bus Routes: 7d, 7b, 10, 11, 11b, 11a, 14, 14a, 15b, 15, 15e
LUAS: Harcourt (Green Line), Jervis (Red Line)
Parking: Hilton Hotel Car Park

U2 locations

U2 Merchandise and Autographs Book and Music Market, Temple Bar Square, Dublin 2 Telephone (Peter): +353 87 2443865 (Outside Ireland) 0872443865 (within Ireland)	Opening Hours Saturday & Sunday 11am-6pm Dún Laoghaire People Park Market Sunday 11am-5pm Bus Routes: 1, 2, 3, 4, 4a, 5, 7, 7d, 7n, 7b,7a, 8 LUAS: Jervis (Red Line), St Stephen's Green (Green Line) DART: Tara Street Parking: Fleet Street Car Park	
Ulster Hall 34 Bedford Street Belfast, BT2 7FF Co. Antrim Telephone: 0044 28 90334400 email: ulsterhall@ belfastcuty.gov.uk Website: www. belfastcity.gov.uk/ ulsterhall		U2 gigged here on 17 December 1980
The Wall of Fame 20 Temple Lane South Temple Bar Dublin 2 Telephone: 01 6709202 Website: www. tbmc.ie		Bus Routes: 1, 2, 3, 4, 4a, 5, 7, 7d, 7n, 7b,7a, 8 LUAS: Jervis (Red Line), St Stephen's Green (Green Line) DART: Tara Street Parking: Fleet Street Car Park
Waterfront 2 Lanyon Place Belfast, BT1 3WH Co. Antrim Telephone: 0044 28 9033 4400 email: enquiries@ waterfront.co.uk Website: www. waterfront.co.uk		U2 performed three songs here in 1998

Westland Studios Magennis Place Dublin 2 Telephone: 01 6779762 or 0879668333 email: westland studios@gmail.com Website: www. westlandstudios dublin.com		*Zooropa* rehearsals were held here Bus Routes: 1, 2, 3, 4a, 4, 5, 7a, 7n, 7d, 7b, 7, 8 LUAS: George's Dock (Red Line) St Stephen's Green (Green Line) DART: Pearse Street Parking: City Quay Car Park
Whelans 25 Wexford Street Dublin 2 Telephone: 01 4780766 Ticket Sales: 1890 200 078 (from Ireland) email: info@ whelanslive.com Website: www. whelanslive.com		Bus Routes: 7d, 7b, 10, 11a, 11, 11b, 14, 14a, 15a, 15f, 15e, 15b LUAS: Harcourt (Green Line). Jervic (Red Line) DART: Pearse Street Parking: Royal College of Surgeons Car Park
Windmill Lane Dublin 2 (U2's old studios: now demolished)		Bus Routes: 1, 2, 3, 4, 4a, 5, 7a, 7.7d, 7b, 7n, 8 LUAS: Mayor Square – NCI (Red Line), St Stephen's Green (Green Line) DART: Pearse Street Parking: IFSC Car Park
The Works Studio 8 Grand Canal Street Upper Dublin 4	Studio where part of Pop was recorded DART: Grand Canal and 200 metres to the left. Bus Routes: Pearse Street/Grand Canal Dock: 1, 2, 3, 50, 56\a, 74, 74a, 77, 77a Grand Canal Street (Mount Street Stop): 4/a, 7, 7a	

Books and websites

Books

Bono (2005) Mick Wall, Carlton
My Boy. The Philip Lynott Story (1995) Philomena Lynott, Hot Press Books
Popaganda: Essential U2 Quotations (2007) Tony Clayton-Lee
Rock Atlas (2011) David Roberts, Clarksdale Books
The Thing Is.... (2010) Dave Fanning, HarperCollins
U2: A Diary (2008) by Matt McGee, Omnibus Press
U2 by U2 by Neil McCormick, HarperCollins
Unforgettable Fire (1987) by Eamon Dunphy, Penguin Publishing Group

Websites

www.u2.com Official U2 Website
www.vertigo-live.com Vertigo – U2 Tribute Band
www.u2gigs.com
List of all gigs performed by U2
www.dublin.ratemyarea.com Allows user look for any place in Dublin, with directions and local amenities

On film

There are many live DVDs of U2 from around the world, but below are a few with particular reference to U2's Dublin.

Michael Collins (1996) Historical drama about the 1916 rising and the man, Michael Collins, who led the country to becoming independent. Gives some idea of the history of Ireland as well as having some scenes shot in Kilmainham Jail/Gaol, where U2 recorded the video for 'A Celebration'.

Rattle and Hum (1988) Documentary following U2 on their Joshua Tree tour. Some new studio songs that appeared on the album *Rattle and Hum*. Shows some venue such as The O2 (Point Depot) where U2 played their New year's Eve gigs in 1989.

It Might Get Loud (2009) Documnetary in which The Edge, Jack White and Jimmy Page discuss their influences, history and memories of music.

The Sky Fall Down (2011) Part of the *Achtung Baby* 20-year anniversary release, this is a documentary on the making of the album.

Albums

U2 3 (EP)	1979
Boy	1980
October	1981
War	1983
Under A Blood Red Sky	1983
The Unforgettable Fire	1984
Wide Awake In America	1986
The Joshua Tree	1987
Rattle and Hum	1988
Achtung Baby	1991
Zooropa	1993
Passengers	1995
Pop	1997
All That You Can't Leave Behind	2000
How To Dismantle An Atomic Bomb	2004
No Line On The Horizon	2009
Songs of Innocence	2014

Singles

Another Day	1980
11 O'Clock Tick Tock	1980
A Day Without Me	1980
I Will Follow	1980
Fire	1981
Gloria	1981
A Celebration	1982
I Will Follow (live)	1982
New Year's Day	1983
Two Hearts Beat As One	1983
Sunday Bloody Sunday	1983
I Will Follow (live)	1984
Pride (In The Name Of Love)	1984
The Unforgettable Fire	1985
With Or Without You	1987
I Still Haven't Found What I'm Looking For	1987
Where the Streets have No Name	1987
In God's Country	1987
One Tree Hill	1988
Desire	1988
Angel Of Harlem	1988
When Love Comes To Town	1989
All I Want Is You	1989
The Fly	1991
Mysterious Ways	1991
One	1992
Even Better Than The Real Thing	1992
Who's Gonna Ride Your Wild Horses	1992
Numb	1993
Lemon	1993
Stay (Faraway So Close)	1993
Hold Me, Thrill Me, Kiss Me, Kill Me	1995
Miss Sarajevo	1995
Discothèque	1997
Staring at the Sun	1997
Last Night on Earth	1997
Please	1997
If God Will Send His Angels	1997
Mofo	1997
Sweetest Thing	1998
Beautiful Day	2000
Stuck In A Moment You Can't get Out Of	2001
Elevation	2001
Walk On	2001
Electrical Storm	2002
Vertigo	2004
All Because Of You	2005
Sometimes You Can't Make It On Your Own	2005
City Of Blinding Lights	2005
One (with Mary J Blige)	2006
The Saints Are Coming (with Green Day)	2006
Window In The Sky	2007
The Ballad Of Ronnie Drew	2008

U2 locations

Get On Your Boots	2009	Ordinary Love	2013
Magnificent	2009	Invisible (Red) Edit Version	2014
I'll Go Crazy If I Don't Go Crazy Tonight	2009	The Miracle (of Joey Ramone)	2014
I will Follow – Live from Glastonbury	2011	Every Breaking Wave	2014

Tour releases

Boy Tour
Live from Boston 1981
(digital album, part of The Complete U2)

War Tour
Live at Red Rocks: Under a Blood Red Sky (video)
Under a Blood Red Sky (album)

The Unforgettable Fire Tour
Wide Awake In America (live and studio EP)

Live Aid
Live Aid and *Live Aid: 20 Years Ago Today* (video)

The Joshua Tree Tour
Rattle and Hum (album and rockumentary film),*Live from Paris* (video available in *The Joshua Tree* box set)

Lovetown Tour
Live from the Point Depot (digital album, part of *The Complete U2*)

Zoo TV Tour
Zoo TV: Live from Sydney (video)
Zoo TV Live (fan club exclusive album)

Stop Sellafield Concert
Stop Sellafield: The Concert (video)

Popmart Tour
Please: PopHeart Live EP (live EP)
PopMart: Live from Mexico City (video)
Hasta la Vista Baby! (fan club exclusive album)

America: A Tribute to Heroes
America: A Tribute to Heroes (album and video)

Elevation Tour
U2: Go Home (live DVD from Slane Castle)
Elevation (Live DVD from Boston

Vertigo Tour
Vertigo (live DVD from Chicago)
U2.COMmunication (fan club exclusive album)
Vertigo 05: Live from Milan (video bundled with deluxe version of U218 Singles)
U2 3D (3D film)

Live 8
Live 8: One Day, One Concert, One World (video)

360° Tour
U2 360 at the Rose Bowl (video)
Wide Awake in Europe (live EP)

U2 Innocence + Experience Tour
U2 Innocence + Experience Tour, Live from Paris

List of Tours

Shown are: the name of tour; year(s) of tour; number of legs; and number of dates

U2-3 Tour (1979–1980; 1; 11)
11 O'Clock Tick Tock Tour (1980; 1; 22)
Boy Tour (1980-1981; 5; 157)
October Tour (1981-1982; 5; 102)
War Tour (1982-1983; 5; 109)
The Unforgettable Fire Tour (1984-1985; 6; 113)
Live Aid (1995; 1; 1)
A Conspiracy of Hope (1986; 1; 6)
The Joshua Tree Tour (1987; 3; 110)
Lovetown Tour (1989-1990; 2; 47)
Zoo TV Tour (1992-1993; 5; 158)
Stop Sellafield Concert (1992; 1; 1)
PopMart Tour (1997-1998; 4; 94)
Elevation Tour (2001; 3; 113)
America: A Tribute to Heroes (2001; 1; 1)
Vertigo Tour (2005-2006; 5; 132)
Live 8 (2005; 1; 1)
U2 360° Tour (2009-2011; 6; 98)
Innocence + Experience (2015; 2; 77)